Praise for *Litera*
The Evolution ~~and Development~~
of Literacy Proficiency

MW01506264

"The authors of this book provide an interesting historical perspective on the concept of literacy and explore many ways literacy has evolved. Given the misinformation and disinformation that have become part of our society, this book is both important and timely.

Literacy in a Digital World: The Evolution and Development of Literacy Proficiency draws the reader's attention to both the similarities and the differences between traditional text and digital media, and in doing so, makes a strong case for all of us to understand better the urgent need to be vigilant when reading texts. This book not only presents educational and psychological theories related to literacy but also provides lessons so that educators can help young adults apply strategies that facilitate the skill of critical thinking as they work to distinguish between factual information and false information within the varied types of texts of today.

This book will help create citizens who understand the importance of learning how to negotiate texts of all sorts in order to create a society that values truth. There is so much relevant information in this book that it demands to be read and re-read." —**Athina-Eleni G. Mavroudhis, former director of psychology and human development, Hellenic College Holy Cross, Brookline, Massachusetts**

"This book presents both the difficulty and the necessity of achieving literary proficiency in a technological age. It describes the evolution of the concept of literacy and the ways it has been assessed over time. Digital texts require readers to develop a sensitivity to language that differs from the way they have traditionally approached paper texts. The authors detail ways in which specific forms of media direct the way readers evaluate messages, and they encourage educators to incorporate media literacy into their teaching processes. This book should be required reading for educators at every level. It is thoroughly researched, expertly presented, and beautifully written." —**Mary E. Robbins, PhD, senior associate to the provost for communication and faculty affairs, University of Massachusetts Lowell**

"It is clear from this book that literacy instruction needs to keep up with advances in technology in a digital world. A clear presentation of the evolution of literacy instruction lays the foundation for the need to adapt literacy instruction and assessment as an ongoing process and to include evaluative literacy as part of this instruction.

The section on assessment is especially helpful, covering different types of assessments and how the principles for assessment presented can guide future work. It demonstrates how media literacy assessment tasks can be more engaging to learners and shows the more authentic ways that digital literacy skills can be assessed at each stage of the assessment process. Student self-assessment with specific guidelines is presented as an important component of the assessment process.

The professional development section shows the forward-thinking needed to address getting educators engaged with these initiatives. Many classroom teachers already see the need for evaluative literacy instruction and assessment revision but may not be as aware of the many recommendations provided by the authors to address current evaluative literacy needs. Possible approaches to effective professional development in media literacy are shared and evaluated, as well as challenges that educators face in transforming literacy instruction in a digital world." — **Kathy Wesley, teacher, Prince George's County Public Schools, Maryland**

Literacy in a Digital World

Literacy in a Digital World

The Evolution and Development of Literacy Proficiency

Lorraine Dagostino, Jennifer Bauer,
Michael Deasy, and Kathleen Ryan

ROWMAN & LITTLEFIELD

Lanham • Boulder • New York • London

Published by Rowman & Littlefield
An imprint of The Rowman & Littlefield Publishing Group, Inc.
4501 Forbes Boulevard, Suite 200, Lanham, Maryland 20706
www.rowman.com

86-90 Paul Street, London EC2A 4NE

British Library Cataloguing in Publication Information Available

Library of Congress Cataloging-in-Publication Data Available

Library of Congress Control Number: 2023948752

ISBN: 978-1-4758-6891-3 (cloth)
ISBN: 978-1-4758-6892-0 (paperback)
ISBN: 978-1-4758-6893-7 (electronic)

♾™ The paper used in this publication meets the minimum requirements of American National Standard for Information Sciences—Permanence of Paper for Printed Library Materials, ANSI/NISO Z39.48-1992.

Contents

Acknowledgments

Writing a book always needs the support of others. For this support, we thank families and friends who gave us the time to do the work. We thank our editors, Tom Koerner and Jasmine Holman, for their guidance in doing this work.

We also thank several people who read the manuscript and made kind remarks in the final days of the writing: Raymond Pape, Mary Robbins, Kathy Wesley, Joe Drolette, and Athina-Eleni Mavroudhis. These people brought to their reading many years of work as educators and, in some instances, parents of young adults. They also brought their experience as life-long readers to the reading.

We now thank you for choosing to read what we believe that we have to offer you.

Introduction

Answering the question, "Why write this book at this time?" points to our curiosity with several concerns. Each of these concerns helps to frame the plan for this book. These concerns are (1) Historical Perspectives, (2) Evaluation of Messages, (3) Digital Literacy, (4) Research, Instruction, and Assessment, (5) Technological Advancements, (6) Professional Development, and (7) Implications and Adaptations. An overview of our concerns may be helpful here.

HISTORICAL PERSPECTIVES

First, understanding the historical perspective on the constantly evolving concept of literacy gives us a good context for addressing the other concerns that shape important discussions. Doing so also leads to understanding the future directions of literacy proficiency, directing the assessment and the development of literacy proficiency. This historical perspective shows how change is inevitable and that we must adapt to it.

EVALUATION OF MESSAGES

Second, understanding the need to constantly evaluate all messaging helps us know what to believe when processing any form of communication. The ability to separate credible messages from misinformation is crucial as the nature of gatekeeping has changed. Evaluating messages sent in any form helps the receiver from being manipulated by others.

DIGITAL LITERACY

Third, the activity with digital literacies pushed the need to explain the evolving concept of literacy to accommodate today's world. This digital work is causing exponential changes in our concept of literacy. This is something that we must address to be prepared for the kinds of communication that we are now facing.

RESEARCH, INSTRUCTION, AND ASSESSMENT

Fourth, the activity surrounding present research and assessment activities forces our hands to understand how classrooms, instruction, and teachers will need to adapt to change continuingly. Our views on assessment must change dramatically to meet the new demands of evaluating success with literacy proficiency. In turn, instruction and assessment must be aligned and integrated as we move forward.

TECHNOLOGICAL ADVANCEMENTS

Fifth, staying abreast of the technological advancements that enhance educational work is crucial to our success. These technologies can improve our work and also require constant relearning to help us adapt to the infrastructures that have developed from their use. We will need to become proficient with technology for day-to-day living and literacy.

PROFESSIONAL DEVELOPMENT

Sixth, what we see about these concerns tells us there is a need for professional development for all educators and instructional and assessment practices. Expecting the implementation of changes requires guidance for all providers of literacy proficiency.

IMPLICATIONS AND ADAPTATIONS

Seventh, constant adaptation is the underlying process that influences our views on literacy as the world of literacy continues to change in a myriad of ways. Without this adaptation, we will be limited in our functioning in the demands of the future – the implications of what we say in this book rest on accepting constant adaptation to continuing change.

Finally, throughout the text, you will see some variation in language concerning reading, readers, and teachers with literacy learners and educators. These variations simply reflect the language used in the literature or our initiatives to broaden the views outlined in this text. We trust you to recognize this aspect of using language for what it represents and not cause confusion.

We hope this book conveys our curiosity about these concerns in a way that makes you think about these inevitable changes in understanding many aspects of literacy so that adaptation is possible and productive.

PART I

LITERACY IN A DIGITAL WORLD

Chapter 1

The Nature of Literacy and Evaluation

OVERVIEW

This chapter traces the changes in how literacy has been viewed and the societal forces that have triggered those changes. The current conceptualization must emphasize the evaluation of messages in traditional and nontraditional forms and technology's role in those evaluations. To accomplish this task, we identify criteria for the evaluation of messages and how to integrate evaluation into the comprehension processes of text.

GUIDING QUESTIONS

How has the concept of literacy changed over time?
What are the triggers for these changes?
What is the concept of evaluative literacy?
How does the concept of evaluative literacy apply to all forms of text?
What are the characteristics of evaluative literacy for all forms of text?
How is the process of evaluation integral to comprehension and all forms of text?

THE EVOLUTION OF THE CONCEPT OF LITERACY IN INTERNATIONAL INITIATIVES TO DEVELOP UNIVERSAL LITERACY

The International Initiatives from 1945 to the Present

Understanding how the concept of literacy has changed over time helps us to see how the present circumstances require the focus on evaluating all kinds of messages that are part of today's communication. So, we begin with a look at these changes and the concept of evaluative literacy to show the importance of integrating evaluation in all text processing.

The evolution of the concept of literacy is represented in the historical progression of efforts to develop worldwide literacy that have occurred since the end of World War II (Dagostino et al., 2016; Deasy, 2012). During that time, there have been five distinct periods of literacy initiatives.

The concept of literacy has evolved from the first-period view, seen as a discrete set of skills or fundamental, basic literacy and a human right, to a second period as a human resource skill for economic growth. The third period emerged as involving the development of the capacities for sociocultural and political change. These were simple but significant changes in the concept that had a great impact on society and schools.

More complex views emerged in the fourth and fifth periods due to intensive global initiatives. The fourth period has been viewed as a combination of the points of view from periods one, two, and three and broadening the perspective with more internationally driven initiatives. Each of these four periods moved from being simple to more complex in nature and more far-reaching in scope.

Finally, the fifth and present period reflects the most complex, widespread concept of literacy that embraces the previous views. A global digital revolution in communication impacts this present view. This period has the concept of literacy that develops a person's potential to engage extensively in social, economic, and political communities in a broadened view of literacy that now embraces a digital world.

First Period: Literacy as a Fundamental Human Right
and Basic Skill: Getting Started 1947–1965

The initial period of international efforts to develop universal literacy commenced with the founding of the United Nations in 1947 and the establishment of the United Nations Educational, Scientific and Cultural Organization (UNESCO). In this period, literacy was promoted as a fundamental human right in the UN Declaration of Human Rights. The definition of literacy in this period was "a literate person is one who can, with understanding, both read and write a short simple statement on his or her everyday life" (UNESCO, 2005, p. 153).

Reflecting this concept, action to promote literacy focused on promoting basic literacy in schools. More specifically, the literacy abilities of the populace consisted of developing the ability to read and write personal pieces such as letters, statements of opinion, or text on a current topic of interest to the general community. Individuals needed to be able to read simple legal documents that confirmed important life transitions. Pleasure reading was included in this definition.

It was assumed that having this level of literacy would protect individual human rights and help people function in the world that was emerging from World War II. However, as the United States and some other parts of the world became more affluent and many people were entering the burgeoning workforce, the need for the concept of literacy to change emerged into what we are considering the second period for the evolution of the concept of literacy—the development of workplace literacy (Sticht & Caylor, 1971; Sticht & Kern, 1970; Sticht, 1995; Sticht, 1975). This context increased the difficulty of achieving literacy as the context for demonstrating skill varied tremendously by becoming specific to the environment where one worked. This impacted the schools (Sticht, 1975).

Second Period: Shifting to Workplace Literacy: 1965–1975

During this second period, the concept of literacy shifted from fundamental literacy to workplace literacy with a focus on training and increasing productivity in the workplace. The second period began in 1965 with the World Congress of Ministers of Education on the Eradication of Illiteracy, Tehran, Iran (UNESCO, 2005). What emerged was a sense that something more was needed for reading and writing skills to be adequate for functioning effectively in the economic world where people now found themselves (Sticht, 1975).

During the second period, the concept shifted to where being literate meant being able to carry out the reading and writing tasks of the workplace. The shift during this period was influenced by the economic condition of a changing society as well as the present needs of the individual. Specifically, these efforts were focused on eleven countries from the four regions of the Middle East, Africa, Asia, and South America over a five-year period (UNESCO, 2005).

In this period, we see the workplace environment requiring greater knowledge of equipment and technical skills in the trades. This, along with the need for new learning and the expansion of the corporate world, pushed for both working class and management development of skills. Workers needed to learn to negotiate for their pay and working conditions. This combined a push for trade skills and college-level education. This had an impact on the schools.

As the second period evolved, further needs emerged. The populace now needed to participate in the world in a more sophisticated way. Individuals needed to recognize the role of literacy in helping them function in a more complex socio-political world. This need helped the movement into the third period, focusing on social and political dimensions of literacy.

Third Period: Expanding to Social and Political
Dimensions of Literacy: 1975–1990

During the third period of this evolution, beginning around 1975 with the International Symposium on Literacy at Persepolis, Iran, the concept of literacy expanded beyond workplace literacy. It included not only the needed basic skills of reading and writing for fundamental and workplace literacy but also the ability to use these skills to function and effect change in social and political worlds (Cassel & Li, 1997).

The international community saw the shift in the definition of literacy from functional literacy to where UNESCO explained literacy as,

> A person is functionally literate who can engage in all those activities in which literacy is required for effective functioning of his group and community and also to use reading, writing and calculation for his own and the community's development. (UNESCO, 2005, p. 154)

The push was for the populace to participate in all aspects of society.

The focus of the thinking that influenced the concept of literacy during this period was socio-political empowerment. People were encouraged to have a prominent voice in community and world affairs. Some initiatives during this period took the form of large-scale mass literacy campaigns to increase universal literacy (Lind, 2008; Arnove & Graff, 1987). The early literacy campaigns influenced the citizenry substantially and focused on developing the populations' awareness of individual and socio-political identities (Cassel & Li, 1997).

Just as this awareness for greater participation became part of the societal concept of literacy, the populace began wanting more. They were looking for the self-actualization suggested by people like Maslow (1987) some years before the emerging fourth period. This self-actualization would influence an individual's and a community's sense of identity and place in the world.

Fourth Period: Combining Personal and Social
Aspects of Literacy: 1990–2009

The fourth period saw both an expansion of the concept of literacy to include new advances in communication technology and a re-association of literacy with the Universal Declaration of Human Rights. This prompted several international initiatives because of greater interaction among key global powers and stronger economic concerns and issues in developing countries. The push for socio-political empowerment continued and spread further worldwide.

This fourth period began around 1990 with the celebration of the International Literacy Year and the World Conference for All at Jomtien, Thailand (UNESCO, 2005). The shift at that time reflected more complexity in the nature of literacy. Reflected in this view, the fourth period also saw a return to the idea of literacy as a basic skill when basic and workplace skills needed to be changed from what was presented in the Universal Declaration of Human Rights to more complex skills.

Being literate meant using reading and writing effectively in a more complex workplace and one's social and political worlds. The combination of previous views meant that many things needed to change in this period's view of literacy in society and schools. As a personal dimension, it was seen as a fundamental human right. In the workplace dimension, it provided tools and skills to engage in the economic life of the local and global communities. In its social and political dimension, it enabled a person to be part of the political and social worlds at local, national, and international levels beyond what was happening in the third period of the evolution of literacy (UNESCO, 2005).

Integrating and synthesizing the multiple international initiatives that were expanding, the International Literacy Year (1990) encouraged the development of reading and writing around the globe. The Literacy Year coincided with the World Conference at Jomtien, Thailand. This conference set out goals for literacy development and promoted the orchestration of the multiple international organizations that were involved in literacy development. The conference forced a broadened view of literacy.

The next major international initiative during this period was the Fifth International Conference on Adult Education, held in Hamburg, Germany, in 1997. This conference integrated the idea that literacy was both a fundamental human right with the idea that literacy was a tool that provided the basic knowledge and skills needed for people to live successfully in a rapidly changing world. Literacy was described at the conference as having a dual role: it was necessary for humans to grow and to develop their full potential along with the foundational skills for one's life (UNESCO, 2005).

The World Economic Forum in Dakar, Senegal, in 2000, followed the Adult Education Conference calling for a 50 percent increase in literacy rates. It established the definition of literacy that the UN would use for the upcoming Literacy Decade.

The definition presented literacy as a complex task with personal and social dimensions, just as the third period did for individuals and communities to become more socially and politically active in increasing their empowerment. It promoted a vision of literacy that was multi-dimensional. For example, its vision of literacy saw people using written communication in ways that strengthened their place in society, gave expression to their identity, facilitated learning, and enabled open and respectful dialogue with neighbors of the local and global communities.

The conference talked about creating a literate community that had multiple literate environments that were self-sustaining and interlocking and led to the expression of three social and personal forms of literacy. These three forms were literacy for democratic participation, "a voice for all," literacy for fulfilling your potential, "learning for all," literacy for expression and sharing of identity and knowledge, and "creative and reciprocal literacies" (UNESCO, 2003).

The Dakar conference paved the way for the establishment of the UN Literacy Decade beginning in 2003. Mirroring the Dakar conference and UNESCO's view of literacy, the Literacy Decade saw literacy as a complex task with strong social-political dimensions. It called for efforts to increase literacy rates by 50 percent. Prompted by this view, the UN called for improving the quality of education by focusing on these five areas:

1. For the UN to be a laboratory for ideas for developing effective literacy practices
2. For the UN to set standards for literacy development
3. For the UN to be a clearing house of ideas for literacy development
4. For the UN to be a capacity building of schools seeking to develop literacy
5. For the UN to be a catalyst for international cooperation

Midway through the Literacy Decade, the UN reported progress toward reaching these goals except in those countries with the lowest literacy rates. As a result, the UN called for more work to aid schools in providing effective literacy instruction, getting more kids attending school, and increasing the focus on helping adults become more literate (UNESCO, 2008).

During this period, to help countries understand their students' performance, two international organizations, the International Association for the Evaluation of Educational Achievement (IEA) and the Organization for Economic Co-operation and Development (OECD), began to administer large-scale literacy assessments. These assessments gave a measure of general achievement and international performance comparisons, reflecting this broadened scope of concerns about literacy.

With this expansion of literacy assessment came the growing world of reading in online environments, with the international assessments incorporating digital literacy tasks in Programme in International Student Assessment's (PISA) work in 2009 and the 2016 version of the PIRLS assessment. This signaled the shift into the fifth period of the evolution of the concept of literacy—the move into the digital environment. The fourth period reflected the movement into the digital world, and the fifth period saw this movement mushroom extensively.

Fifth Period: Expanding in a Digital World: 2009 to Present

The fifth period in this evolution represents a shift in the definition of literacy into reading and writing in the digital world, specifically online/digital environments. The definition extends the definition of literacy from the fourth period to include the complex, evaluative tasks that readers and writers must do as they navigate this online/digital environment.

Marking this period in 2009 was the international reading assessment, the PISA, assessing fifteen-year-olds in reading, math, and science by beginning to administer a portion of their reading assessment in a format that simulated online reading environments (OECD, 2021; OECD, 2022).

Here, on a large-scale international reading assessment, students were given reading tasks in a simulated online reading environment and were asked to perform the tasks as they were reading online (OECD, 2021; OECD, 2022). Students were asked to read and navigate simulated web pages while retrieving and interpreting the information that was found. Students also were asked to evaluate search results and make decisions about which website links to follow to attain the information they were seeking (OECD, 2021; OECD, 2022).

PISA began to include these tasks in response to the growth in online reading that students were experiencing at school and in their personal lives (in and out of school). The section on online reading skills was also included because of the recognition that workplace literacy skills were beginning to call for online reading skills (OECD, 2021; OECD, 2022).

The definition that PISA used in the 2009 assessment reflected the view of the fourth period and the recognition of the move into the online, digital space of the fifth period. Their definition was, "Reading literacy is understanding, using, reflecting on and engaging with written texts, in order to achieve one's goals, to develop one's knowledge and potential, and to participate in society" (OECD, 2021). The view of written texts expanded in 2009 to include digital texts such as those found in online reading. "The phrase 'written texts' is meant to include all those coherent texts in which language is used in its graphic form: hand-written, printed and electronic" (OECD, 2021).

The PISA instrument marked the use of an assessment tool for digital work and moved the thinking by schools and organizations to consider the significance of including digital work, both instructional and assessment, for future work such as the 2016 PIRLS work.

Within this fifth period in 2016, the Progress in International Reading Literacy Assessment (PIRLS) began offering e-PIRLS, which includes a section on reading/writing in a simulated online world for fourth-grade students. The fifth period also includes three phases of online activities beyond assessment. They are accessing information, creating content, and navigating a virtual world, particularly social media, marketing goods and services, and online educational opportunities, all extensions and accelerations of the fourth period. This fifth period also was affected by an unexpected trigger of the COVID pandemic that accelerated much online activity.

e-PIRLS

The e-PIRLS assessment was an additional assessment that countries could have their students take while taking the traditional paper-based PIRLS assessment. Here, on a large-scale standardized international reading assessment, students were given reading tasks in a simulated online environment. They were asked to perform reading tasks as if they were reading online.

Students were called upon to select appropriate websites to complete their task (purpose of reading) to comprehend successfully a variety of online texts and text features, navigate through a website and evaluate search results and the author's purpose for creating online material. Two aspects of these tasks that stand out in the definition that PIRLS used are how the definition incorporates the importance of reading multiple texts and the importance of evaluation in the literacy process when reading online.

On the 2016 e-PIRLS assessment, students were asked to perform a simulated online research task. The task involved navigating 3 websites, reading 5–10 pages, and approximately 1,000 words of online text. Along with answering comprehension questions about what they read on the websites, including inferences, interpreting charts and diagrams, and locating and retrieving facts, the students were asked to perform evaluative tasks of determining which website links to follow to obtain the information about the topic and the author's point of view (TIMSS & PIRLS International Study Center, 2022).

It was here that the definition of literacy evolved to be "Reading Literacy is the ability to understand and use written language forms required by society and/or valued by the individual. Readers can construct meaning from texts in a variety of forms. They read to learn, to participate in communities of readers in school and everyday life, and for enjoyment" (Mullis & Martin, 2019). This definition incorporates reading in a variety of forms (digital), and the PIRLS assessment calls on students to "read, interpret and critique" online information (Mullis & Martin, 2019).

In the 2021 version of PIRLS, the instrument offered countries the option of taking PIRLS in a paper-based or digital format. The digital format involved the same tasks as the paper-based version, but the material was presented on the computer, and the students answered the questions on the computer. Countries also had the option to administer the e-PIRLS part of the assessment, exploring how students read and researched in online formats. The 2021 version of the PIRLS followed the same format as the 2016 inaugural version in which students read, researched, and navigated through a simulated online environment.

BEYOND ASSESSMENT INITIATIVES: THREE PHASES OF ONLINE/DIGITAL TASKS

Marking 2016 as the beginning of this fifth period when the international assessment PIRLS began to assess online reading skills and strategies, this period has evolved with three phases that continued and moved the fourth period forward. The phases represent the evolution in the online world of the complex notion of literacy and the importance of evaluation in literacy.

The phases are (1) accessing and reading in online environments—by entering the World Wide Web, (2) creating content in online environments by extending to Web 2.0, and (3) navigating a digital world such as social media to achieve the literacy goals of acquiring content knowledge, creating content and individual communications.

Phase 1—Accessing Information

In phase 1, students engaged in reading online by using search engines to discover websites for the topics that they wanted information about. Here, they evaluated which sites would best provide the information they wanted and constructed an understanding of the topic based on what they read on the websites. During this phase, readers navigated a variety of online texts and text formats while reading.

Phase 2—Content Creation

During the second phase, students gained the ability to interact with the online world in creating creative ways to develop text. Individuals began not only to consume online content but also to create and construct their own online content. This phase, generally referred to as Web 2.0, opened the world for readers to create text online. The formats began to grow: blogs, websites, video blogs, and picture sharing as the technology expanded. This phase involved readers evaluating not only what they would place in the online environment but also what others created in the online environment.

Phase 3—Navigating the Web

The third phase of the fifth period is characterized by the rise of social media and the accelerated marketing of goods and services. Individuals can now interact with others, gain information, and be content creators in the online/digital world in various formats and platforms: Facebook, Twitter, Instagram, text messages, Zoom meetings, Google Meets, and more. These interactions give us a retrievable and decontextualized written communication of our lives.

Part of navigating the web came an increase in the use of online services for marketing goods and services, which had started in the fourth period. With people being busier with social activities and everyday needs came a need for more convenience in shopping for gifts, banking services, general comparative shopping, and faster delivery of items and services. Life began pushing an expectation of instantaneousness. Fraud and scams multiplied too.

Many newscasts are becoming headlines reporting with the need to access complete stories at separate websites. Advertising of goods and services often permeates much of navigating these sites. More online educational opportunities with the completion of degree programs are being offered online to accommodate changing lifestyles and to increase markets to attract larger and more diverse student populations.

These aspects of online environments will continue to grow exponentially. This phase has increased the need for readers not only to navigate these sites but also to successfully evaluate what they encounter when they engage in reading and writing in online/digital environments. Further, this fifth period was hit with an unexpected trigger: COVID-19.

An Unexpected Trigger: COVID-19

In addition to the changing technology from the fourth period, this fifth period saw an unexpected trigger that increased the need for working in a digital world. This trigger event was the COVID-19 pandemic which had its greatest impact in 2020. The world was sent into a tailspin that pushed many learning and work environments into greater remote communication and more social isolation.

Schools and workplaces needed to shift the way they functioned so that they could continue their activity. This forced many individuals into using many types of technology and digital communication that they had not used previously. As these changes happened, we saw more hybrid models of interaction arise. Some of the changes are now becoming the norm.

When the pandemic began to subside, these changes were residual effects that caused an integration of these technological tools into many peoples' environments. This integration of these tools made many of these forced changes part of the evolving concept of literacy for reading professionals and international organizations.

Reading Professionals and International Organizations

As we see the concept of literacy evolving, we see reading professionals and international organizations rethinking their definitions of literacy. Reading professionals incorporate more strongly the variety of online environments that students/individuals process text in now, as well as the increased need to evaluate what is read in the online environment. One expression of this evolution is, "Today, the definition of literacy has expanded from traditional notions of reading and writing to include the ability to learn, comprehend, and interact with technology in a meaningful way" (Selfe cited in Coiro, 2003, p. 458).

In addition to the concept of literacy given by reading professionals, international organizations also expanded their definition of literacy. The United Nations began to include digital literacy in their projects to develop universal literacy (Law et al., 2018). The 2018 definition developed by UNESCO for their international development projects holds that "digital literacy is the ability to access, manage, understand, integrate, communicate, evaluate and create information safely and appropriately through digital technologies for employment, decent jobs, and entrepreneurship" (Law et al., 2018). The hope is that these evolved concepts filter into society and the educational institutions that present crucial information and ideas to create informed citizens.

NAEP and the Future of the Concept of Literacy

We return to literacy assessment here because assessments such as NAEP— the National Assessment for the United States, are developing a new reading assessment framework. The framework will be used on the 2026 NAEP assessment and will not only reflect reading in an online environment but also help educators guide students in taking this form of assessment.

On the NAEP 2026 Reading Framework, we see that diverse populations will be provided with an interactive support system while taking the assessment instrument. The supportive elements include text-to-speech directions and help screens, sequential directions, and transitions for reading a collection of texts. There will be graphic organizers along with other support mechanisms. In some instances, some of the support mechanisms may appear more instructional than assessment and thus raise questions about the test being primarily a measure of successful literacy. A definition by NAEP may be helpful here:

According to the NAEP draft framework, reading comprehension is described as

> Reading comprehension is making meaning with text, a complex process shaped by many factors, including readers' abilities to: Engage with text in print and multimodal forms; Employ personal resources that include foundational reading skills, language, knowledge and motivations; and Extract, construct, integrate, critique, and apply meaning in activities across a range of social and cultural contexts. This definition applies to the assessment of reading achievement on NAEP and is not intended to be an inclusive definition of reading instruction. (US Dept. of Education, 2021)

This framework reflects not just measurable aspects of evaluating success in attaining literacy in the future but also those aspects of literacy that sometimes elude us.

We have used PISA, PIRLS, and NAEP to illustrate the changes occurring in assessment instruments. However, this does not diminish the contributions of other assessments such as UNESCO-2018 (Antoninis & Montoya, 2018), ITU-2018 (Coward & Fellow, 2018), OECD-2016 (OECD, 2015), World Bank-2020 (Blom et al., 2020), and European Union-2016 (European Commission, 2016). The changes in assessment reflected in all of these assessment tools guide our work in assessment and instruction later in this book.

What we have seen in this presentation of the evolution of the concept of literacy is a substantial expansion in language and thinking skills for the populace to achieve proficiency in literacy. It also brings a considerable change in assessment that may drive the concept of literacy and, in turn, instruction. The hope is that we are up to the task.

The fifth period is still evolving beyond what we have presented here. It is bringing not only the expansion of the variety of texts that we will encounter but also a deepening need to evaluate that material so that an individual can construct an effective understanding of the world through both traditional text forms and those in the digital world.

The remaining part of this chapter starts to present how we can begin thinking about reaching this goal. It accomplishes the task by focusing on the concept of evaluative literacy, its characteristics, the attributes of the evaluative individual, and finally, a model of the evaluative process of text.

THE CONCEPT OF EVALUATIVE LITERACY

The Goals of Evaluative Literacy

A primary goal of evaluative literacy is finding the message and evaluating its worth. To accomplish this goal, individuals first, must understand statements literally; second, know how to infer from the details; third, know when to see the role of purpose or motive in influencing the author's stated intentions and tone; and fourth, recognize the assumptions implicit in the message. Doing this should lead to a justifiable interpretation and evaluation of the text (Dagostino & Carifio, 1994; Dagostino, 2019).

Questions and Processing for the Evaluation of Text

Individuals must be able to answer questions such as "What and why is it being said?" and "What is its significance and its relevance to the point being made?" Answering these questions helps the individual find the explicit and the implicit messages in a text. Answering questions such as "How does the presentation of information or ideas influence decision-making?" "What is gained from full disclosure, concealment, or distortion of the facts?" and "Are there omissions or misrepresentations of details?" helps the individual tie the author's purpose or motive to the persuasion used, along with the selection and representation of the details presented.

Such questions are necessary for evaluating a message to make a judgment or a decision because they consider the effects of purpose or motive on the presentation of the message. They suggest recognizing the presentation's influence on the individual's interpretation and evaluation of the response. Questions such as, "What is the logic of the thinking supporting the text?" "Does the writer have strong beliefs or positions on the issue?" "How is this reflected in the unstated assumptions?" "Would other assumptions lead the individual to a different judgment or decision?" are important to good evaluations of a text.

Processing text to make judgments or decisions means there is a goal of determining the merits of a plan, the value of a product, the worth of an individual, or the significance of an idea. The question "What is at stake?" is significant. It sets the degree of objectivity, the latitude of selected criteria, and the stringency of applying criteria for the judgment. Questions such as, "What are you trying to establish?" "How do you work through the process of evaluation?" "When have your hypotheses been verified?" are important not only when a decision or judgment is made but also when the individual considers how the evaluation process influences the decision.

The process applied, or the questions about the content may differ for poetry, essays, stories, scientific pieces, or historical treatises (LeBlanc & Dagostino, 2015). However, getting the message and evaluating its worth remains central to the processing of any kind of material. What makes the task challenging and worth doing is finding both the explicit and implicit messages and the implications in various kinds of texts. This is true, especially for texts that require the individual to move from literal meaning to figurative, symbolic, metaphorical, and abstract expression. This is challenging because the individual is considering the subtext of the text.

To accomplish this task with narrative, individuals must move from understanding character and events to plot, theme, and perspective, processing the language used to create and sustain the metaphors. In exposition, individuals must move from details to issues, to argument, and from text details to trends or patterns (Dagostino & Carifio, 1999, 1995). Synthesizing the details of all kinds of text to understand the topic or the text's theme characterizes the mature reader. Reflecting upon the details of the message helps individuals draw valid conclusions. Being able to transform the process of evaluation for different texts identifies mature individuals.

Mature Individuals' Judgments

Mature individuals think about their purpose for reading and their position on specific issues, knowing that the quality, the direction, and the degree of objectivity in their thinking may be influenced by that purpose or position. Mature individuals know that their purpose first triggers the depth of understanding needed, second the choice of selected criteria for the evaluation, and finally, the stringency of applying the criteria given the significance of the judgments to be made. How objective they remain relates not only to their position on the topic, but also to their ability to reason and "counter-reason."

Guided by the goal of making judgments and decisions, mature individuals also integrate information and ideas from multiple sources as a means of synthesizing different perspectives on a topic or issue. This process helps them broaden their conceptualization of a topic as well as understand how the perspective of each source filters data differently. Mature individuals see how a point of view represents the facts or influences an interpretation of a message. Understanding this, they are better equipped to reconcile diverse points of view and make judgments or decisions about the text.

The mature individual's decisions about a purpose or goal determine how much time to invest, what, and how many criteria to apply. What is at stake in the decision-making determines how much of a need there is to make critical judgments. Once the decision about what is at stake is made, individuals apply the appropriate criteria to evaluate the text. These criteria, often discussed as skills, are strategies in the form of lists or taxonomies. They represent the goals, the expectations, and the process of finding and evaluating the text objectively. They help individuals make a reasoned judgment of the message (Dagostino & Carifio, 1994).

Preceding the application of criteria, however, it is important to determine the attitude toward the topic, the issue, and the form of presentation. This is a way of integrating attitude and criteria to develop expectations. The next sections consider attitudes in relationship to the concept of evaluative literacy.

Viewing Evaluating Text as an Attitude and an Intellectual Act

An individual's decision about a book's value often reveals personal feelings or tastes instead of a judgment guided by external criteria. This suggests that some believe that evaluating text means deciding if they like a text rather than if they think it is good. This may occur for several reasons. First, individuals may not take the time necessary to complete a systematic evaluation of a text. Second, individuals who read primarily to satisfy personal needs may believe such evaluation interferes with their enjoyment of the text. Their purposes for processing, such as escape, or confirmation of a personal view, are contradicted by reflection and evaluation.

However, lacking time and satisfying only personal needs does not justify making decisions about a text's value on personal, subjective criteria only. The two reasons offered here to explain some individuals' acceptance of primarily personal responses to a text are not sufficient. Unfortunately, these reasons may hide the less obvious but more crucial reasons for an individual's reliance on personal feelings or taste. Other reasons that focus on what individuals know about how to process text, how individuals perceive the ability to process text evaluatively, and the merits of doing so may give us less obvious but more helpful explanations.

First, individuals may not know how to process and respond more objectively. That is, they do not know what to look for when asked to be less personal and less subjective in their critique. Not wanting to reveal what they don't know or don't want to learn, their attempts to respond objectively fail.

Second, individuals may not have recognized the need or the merit and the pleasure of a thorough, evaluative processing of a text. Instead, they rely on others for such evaluation. Surrogates help them decide which contracts to sign, how to vote on significant issues, and how to interpret literature and the reports of discoveries.

Third, they simply may have a limited concept of evaluative literacy. Believing that evaluative literacy is an effort that leads only to unpleasant comments or exchanges and to negative judgments, they avoid it. They hide behind believing that they are not suited to such evaluation because they do not like or are not good at conveying criticisms constructively.

Missing from this limited concept of evaluating text is the understanding that evaluation is both a personal and objective response to the text and does not necessarily lead to a negative judgment. Processing text evaluatively is an interaction of attitude, knowledge, and reflection that should lead to a reasoned, objective judgment of written material. Evaluating a text is a positive, reflective act.

Recognizing a Broadened View

Recognizing the need for a broadened view, we accept that for many individuals processing text evaluatively becomes a process of learning to process meaning. From their relearning, individuals will find that evaluation is problem-detecting, searching for ideas, assumptions, and claims, as well as structure in text.

Individuals learn that text is dynamic, and they have the power and the freedom to respond to text rather than simply process and recall it. Individuals will see that the text, which looks so permanent, is a negotiable message. It is a message that should be perceived as a dialogue between the author and the audience.

The implication is that the text is open to question and interpretation, requiring the individual to consider how and where they fit into the exchange. Are they an outsider looking into another exchange? Are they a receiver expected to respond to the ideas or simply accept them as orders? This means that the individual must be able to construct an opposing view or at least a different one from the author; otherwise, the author can persuade the individual to accept the author's point of view and corresponding inclinations or implications too easily.

Processing text evaluatively gives individuals greater power by making them aware of both the necessity and the influence of interpretation. Individuals do not feel trapped by the written word because they know they can make suggestions for change or improvement. Changing words and restricting the thinking of others lets readers use the written text, transfer ideas, and finally transform their thinking on the subject.

An individual's thinking about the text also must be guided by tentativeness and hypothesis-testing before conclusions are drawn. Conclusions also may be seen as open to modification. The individual's attitude toward a balance between tentativeness and conclusiveness directs his/her response toward constant hypothesis-testing and rethinking. The individual gathers details guided by hypotheses.

Understanding and functioning related to tentativeness may encourage conditional thinking (If-then) and suppositional thinking (Suppose that). Such thinking may lead to breaking away from present views, forms of thought, and concepts on different topics. Understanding the tentativeness of text in a changing society is crucial for discussing issues and making informed decisions. Dialogue, spoken or written, is necessary because it moves ideas forward so that a dialectic forms—one that truly tests opposing points of view.

Two theoretically opposing views on a subject are argued and critiqued; a dialectic forms and the synthesis emerges into a new form, concept, or viewpoint. The response to the synthesis sets the cycle in motion again, at least for as long as a decision does not have to be made. Once an action, such as a vote, must occur, the debate and the dialectic cease, and evaluation is made.

Achieving this broadened view of evaluating text may be difficult because practices in many schools, and life in general, more often reward remembering and recalling what is in a text almost verbatim rather than determining the merits of what the individual is being asked to process. Individuals must change their approach and their application of skills to one of acceptance, reflection, learning, and depth of understanding. This means being open. It means considering the author's message before judging or drawing a conclusion.

It means letting your guard down on sensitive topics or keeping your guard up when evaluating overly convincing views on a topic. It means being receptive to ideas. It means that an individual is sure they understand the intentions of the author and that they have given them thought. It means that individuals must learn to remove their skepticism on first reading, keep the content in mind, and return to question systematically the information, the idea, and the point of view presented in the writing. It means recognizing how any bias influences the interpretation.

Extending One's Thinking

If the individual can remain open, processing text evaluatively also means learning more about a subject. Individuals evaluate what they know in light of the text, and vice versa. They decide what is new, what is different, or what is another angle on the topic. They consider when ideas or information can be assimilated directly. Should the individuals' information or concept change? Is the processing effective enough to feel like you are experiencing the situation or problem directly? This processing stretches individuals intellectually by testing what they believe or know and extending their background.

Processing text evaluatively means integrating one's personal view of the world with a broader one. This requires applying standards to judge, justify, or reason about actions and events. This requires analysis and synthesis of the content and the form of the text. Processing text evaluatively also forces individuals to differentiate between opinion, judgment, and justification. Aulls (1982) discusses a range of responses such as opinion, values, judgment, justifiable choice, and argued logical response. He also suggests that responses derived from values-based feelings are broader and less likely to lead to one correct response than those of an argued logical position.

In contrast, evaluations requiring judgments, justified choices, and argued logical positions, although more narrow, imply that some responses are better than others. The correctness of a response depends upon how well it meets some predetermined criteria and how directly it follows from the information in the text. Processing text evaluatively rests upon both types of responses, the ultimate goal being the reasoned judgment where all factors have been considered.

Processing text evaluatively may lead to a rejection of the content and the form of the text. Sometimes, however, it can lead to changed minds or feelings or perhaps simply confirm what individuals already know about a topic. When decisions or judgments are about moral dilemmas, both logic and values interact for the evaluation to occur.

Good evaluations come from suspending judgment about characters, events, conclusions, and values until the details and ideas presented have been weighed objectively. Having patience and reflecting upon details helps with predicting outcomes—yet maintains a needed willingness to shift one's thinking as new information becomes available or before conclusions must be drawn.

To make this general conceptualization useful for objective evaluation, we turn to specific criteria for evaluating all text types. To do this task, we first identify twenty characteristics for evaluating both traditional and nontraditional types of text. Then we consider additional characteristics to evaluate nontraditional text, media, and digital communication.

The Characteristics of Evaluative Literacy

The Characteristics of Evaluative Literacy provide the immediate framework for the instructional and assessment guidelines presented later in this book. So that you will have a sense of each of the twenty characteristics, we will describe them briefly as they were defined for the teachers who tested the validity of these definitions and these plans. We also present additional characteristics for venues beyond the traditional text that these twenty characteristics were derived from. Although initially, this work focused on reading, it also applies to all of the forms of text that we discuss in this book (Dagostino & Carifio, 1994).

There are twenty characteristics in all, and although we have been able to distinguish them from each other, please remember that they may not be mutually exclusive categories. Therefore, there may be some overlap in the sample generic lessons. Again, these characteristics apply beyond traditional text. They also will be enhanced with additional ones that apply to other forms of text (figure 1.1).

The additional characteristics are for electronic, digital, and media text. They have been based upon those used in various class instructions to test their value and usefulness. They, like the previous twenty characteristics, guide the development of instruction, sample lessons, and assessment guidelines presented later in this book.

The 20 Characteristics of Evaluative Reading

1. Reader's General Approach To Text

2. Reading For Intention and Assumptions

3. Reading Different Kinds of Material Evaluatively

4. Establishing Purpose In Reading Evaluatively

5. Teaching How To Read For Point of View

6. Determining Attitude Toward Reading

7. Sorting Personal Feelings From Applications of External Criteria

8. Constructing A Point Of View

9. Drawing Conclusions, Making Predictions and Suspending Judgment Through Maintaining Tentativeness and Hypothesis-Testing

10. The Effects of Interpretation As A Preliminary Step To Evaluation

11. Integrating The Reader's Personal Views With The Views of The Larger World

12. Understanding That Reading Comprehension is a a process of Gathering, Assimilating, Thinking and Restructuring

13. Establishing Reader's Goals

14. Detecting Deception

15. Seeking Credibility and Validity

16. Developing Sensitivity To Language

17. Building Knowledge Bases

18. Developing Schema For Reflective Questioning

19. Achieving Automaticity of Analysis

20. Generating Response To Texts

Figure 1.1   Characteristics of Evaluative Reading.

The twenty characteristics consist of the following:

1. *Reader's General Approach to Text*

   The individual's approach to text includes activating prior knowledge, ensuring openness to the author's message, explicitly stating the individual's knowledge and beliefs about the topic, and testing the message against experiences, logic, and other sources.

2. *Reading for Intention and Assumptions*

   This means comprehending implicit and explicit messages and testing the plausibility of the individual's conclusions. Part of determining explicit and implicit messages means ascertaining the writer's assumptions about the topic and generating other possible assumptions, either complementary or contradictory.

3. *Reading Different Kinds of Material Evaluatively*

   Entails understanding how the evaluation process is transformed for poetry, narrative, exposition, and argumentation by using specific criteria for formal evaluation.

4. *Establishing Purpose in Processing Evaluatively*

   Entails establishing purposes beyond getting literal and basic inferential meaning. Instead, the individual focuses on understanding intentions, assumptions, and themes.

5. *Teaching How to Determine a Point of View*

   Entails understanding that a point of view represents and interprets events and statements differently. This applies to fiction and nonfiction.

6. *Determining Attitude Toward the Text*

   An individual must recognize how they feel about a topic, types of material, styles of writing, and specific points of view because attitude determines how you interact with the ideas and the message and your level of disagreement.

7. *Sorting Personal Feelings from Application of External Criteria*

   An individual needs to know how emotional responses differ from intellectual responses by identifying the "criteria" of emotional response and the "criteria" of objectivity.

8. *Constructing a Point of View*

   An individual needs to understand how having a point of view logically leads to certain actions and reactions.

9. *Drawing Conclusions, Making Predictions, and Suspending Judgment through Maintaining Tentativeness and Hypothesis-Testing.*

   This characteristic is an information-gathering process that requires the individual to bring details to closure periodically, withhold personal judgment, and set the direction for thinking that predicts what will occur.

Logic and information must direct the predictions and the conclusions for a plausible ending to be legitimized.

10. *The Effects of Interpretation as a Preliminary Step to Evaluation*

    This requires understanding how multiple interpretations help to create the openness to message that is necessary for evaluations. Seeing that interpretation influences how external criteria are applied and accepted.

11. *Integrating the Individual's Personal Views with the Views of the Larger World*

    An individual's personal views may be limited or misconceived in relationship to the views of the world at large. This characteristic focuses on the need to compare and synthesize views based on multiple views.

12. *Understanding That Comprehension Is a Process of Gathering, Assimilating, Thinking, and Restructuring*

    An individual views comprehension as an interactive process using skills and strategies to find explicit and implicit meaning. The individual is thinking about the meaning and how they arrived at it so that an appropriate response can be made. This means using (1) determining the importance of information, (2) summarizing text, (3) drawing inferences, (4) generating questions, and (5) monitoring comprehension to achieve a mature response.

13. *Establishing an Individual's Goals*

    Several questions help the individual determine the author's perspective. These questions are (1) What is the author's point of view?, (2) How does s/he establish it?, and (3) what is their purpose? An individual always aims to determine what the writer has to say. Understanding the author's point of view and purpose leads to making a reasonable interpretation of the text. Recognizing how the writer accomplishes their goal helps the individual evaluate the message. Once purpose and point of view are established, a response can be made.

14. *Detecting Deception*

    This facet of processing evaluatively focuses on recognizing propaganda and whether it sells something or someone of value. When the purpose is to persuade, the individual must recognize the writer's slant of information and ideas. The individual must recognize the situational purpose of a text and weigh the message and the presentation.

15. *Seeking Credibility and Validity*

    This dimension of processing evaluatively focuses on distinguishing Fantasy from Reality or Fact from Opinion based on authenticity, adequacy, and relevance, as well as logic and argument. It entails recognizing the influence of beliefs and attitudes that are part of a person's moral structures and knowing what to believe or to do. Doing this means determining the truth unbiased by moral views of an issue. Individuals are looking for plausibility and possibility of the occurrence of events as well as internal validity.

16. *Developing Sensitivity to Language*

This aspect of processing evaluatively focuses on diction, denotation and connotation, tone, figurative language, and use of syntax. Individuals must become sensitive to the framing of a message and what words are chosen to create a particular tone. Additional features are formal or informal register, symbolic or abstract language, and the overall effect of phrasing and sentence structure.

17. *Building Knowledge Bases*

This aspect of processing evaluatively focuses on building general knowledge for different established bodies of knowledge on different topics. It entails building points of comparison to test ideas in a text and building bases for the assimilation and accommodation of new information and ideas.

18. *Developing Schema for Reflective Questioning*

Individuals must learn to monitor comprehension by questioning themselves and the text in a reflective manner.

19. *Achieving Automaticity of Analysis*

Individuals must automate all of the skills and strategies they have developed so that analysis and evaluation are assimilated into the habits and processes they take to the text.

20. *Generating Response to Texts*

This dimension of processing focuses on an individual's response to text beyond basic literal and inferential comprehension along the lines of the following chart (figure 1.2).

The twenty characteristics defined here may not be mutually exclusive of each other, but they can be developed as part of an overall strategy for encouraging individuals to be more evaluative and reflective about the material that they process. This means that in some cases, an individual lesson may address more than one characteristic at a time in other instances, it may not do so. The overriding goal, however, is to focus the individual's attention on a kind of thinking and processing that often are not part of their regular approach to the text.

Additional Characteristics for Other Venues

As we have progressed into the digital age, more nuanced definitions of these evaluative characteristics are needed. Although the media has changed our landscape, the evaluative tools needed to understand, interpret, delineate, and analyze messages have not. What has changed is the application of these

Awareness of Human Experiences and Dilemmas	Social Sensitivity
	Empathy
	Tolerance
	Openness

Responsible Communication of Individual and Collective Thought	Schemas	Shared Knowledge
		Informed Opinions & Decisions
	Cognitive Activities	Questioning
		Systematic Inquiry
		Specialized Schemas
	Judicious Thoughts	Selection of Appropriate Forms of Communications
		Flexibility in Language and Thinking
	Aesthetic Forms	Creative Expression
		Eloquence of Language
		Metaphoric Thinking

Figure 1.2   The Outcomes of Literacy (Dagostino, 1987).

characteristics. We still need to understand how to process different kinds of materials evaluatively. Here, we address four of the applicable characteristics of other venues:

- Detecting Deception
- Seeking Credibility and Validity
- Developing Sensitivity to Language
- Algorithms

Detecting Deception: These days, digital media, particularly video, audio, photography, and social media, have made deception easier to propagate and much more difficult to identify. For example, the technology used to create deep fake videos (videos of people speaking that are not real) is well-developed. It is becoming exceedingly hard to identify real versus fake. Social media plays a role in deception by allowing people to quickly and easily spread misinformation and disinformation.

The same evaluative concerns apply to these new media, with some additions. One needs to understand the effects of sound effects and music, as well as visual editing, such as pacing and the pairing of disparate images, and how these techniques can alter the perception of a message. Video and audio can create a stronger emotional response than text alone.

Seeking Credibility and Validity: Again, this is more difficult in the age of new media. Graphics and animations create a sense of authority that doesn't necessarily exist. Additionally, many online platforms use hyperlinks to send users to other sources of information and websites. Hyperlinks add another layer of analysis, as each linked source needs to be evaluated for credibility and validity.

Questions one must ask are, "Who's behind this information? What's the evidence? What do other outlets say?" It is easy for anyone to publish information online, creating a website or news article that looks credible. No longer is information coming only from trusted media outlets and written by trained journalists adhering to the ethical standards of their profession. This makes it even more important to understand how to identify credible, valid information.

Developing Sensitivity to Language: Headlines online are VERY different than in print sources for two reasons: *SEO* (search engine optimization) – Google loves headlines full of search terms and *clickbait*. These are headlines written to sell, not tell, the story. Memes are another example of how we need to develop our sensitivity to language. They are a remixing of videos and images that take on new shared meanings. Understanding their origins and evolution is key to evaluating their messages.

Algorithms: Finally, we need to understand how we are being manipulated, particularly by algorithms used by search engines and social media platforms that tailor the information we see. Instead of providing a balance of sources and information, algorithms reinforce our beliefs. These are complex calculations used by search engines and social media tools that analyze the information we seek and then tailor our results in subsequent searches only to include results that reflect our previous searches. Unless one actively seeks information outside of this filter bubble, they will be more likely only to see information that reflects their values and beliefs.

How Things Work

From a theoretical point of view, we can see the explanations about the evaluation process and the nature of the evaluative individual by examining two models. The first model is that of the evaluative individual of all texts (Dagostino & Carifio, 1994). The second one is that of the evaluative processes as an integral part of comprehension and evaluation of text and messages regardless of the form of text. These models follow in the next two sections of Chapter One (Dagostino, 1991).

Attributes of Literate Individuals

Here, we turn to the first model of the Attributes of the Evaluative Individual (figure 1.3) (Dagostino & Carifio, 1994).

The acceptance of the idea that evaluation of text is a primary goal in achieving literacy raises the question of the attributes of the evaluative individual. And how do they face and focus on various types of text? We have begun to address these questions in previous parts of the chapter but wish to share a model that explains further this aspect of the topic.

The evaluative individual possesses several attributes that contribute to the interactive process of evaluative literacy. They, in turn, are interactive components of the model that is represented in the figure that follows. Specifically, there are four major attributes in this model. They are (1) *maturity*, (2) *attitudes and dispositions,* (3) *intellectual abilities,* and (4) *knowledge and experience.* The dominant attribute is maturity because it is a psychologically developmental factor that encompasses and affects the other three attributes (Dagostino & Carifio, 1994).

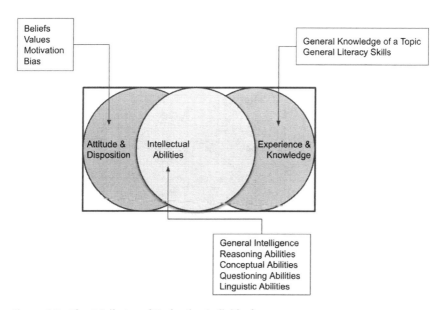

Figure 1.3 The Attributes of Evaluative Individual.

More specifically, maturity is the progressive development from egocentric thinking to group transcendence. This is part of the reason for beginning instruction in evaluative literacy in the middle grades. This is the time to prepare individuals to develop less egocentric worldviews. Developing the maturity that allows individuals to see topics, ideas, or issues from different points of view is difficult, but it is an important goal in teaching evaluative literacy. It is a gradual process that should be started early.

In addition to the attribute of maturity, we also must consider how the attitudes and the dispositions of an individual influence comprehension. An interpretation of a text depends on the degree of receptiveness, openness, and broadmindedness the individual brings to the text. Without this fairness of mind, interpretation will likely remain egocentric and narrow, possibly missing the author's message completely. Therefore, it is crucial as a part of assessing one's own attitudes and disposition, an individual is clear about their beliefs, values, motivation, and interests as well as bias on a particular subject or issue. We distinguish these factors as follows:

1. *Beliefs*—views held with or without evidence to support their validity
2. *Values*—positions and priorities of importance
3. *Motivation and Interests*—forces that propel the pursuit of a topic, issue, problem, or goal
4. *Bias*—a particular slant or position on an issue

Attitudes and dispositions set the frame of reference for approaching a text, and they must include the ability to balance emotional and intellectual predispositions and responses to ideas and information for objective processing to occur.

Next, the evaluation of text often depends upon aspects of intellectual ability, where this ability is broadly defined as the abilities that contribute to the individual's ability to think. This, too, may be a developmental issue. The intellectual abilities that are part of our model are:

1. *General Intelligence*—the capacity to observe and to infer, to synthesize and to apply knowledge
2. *Conceptual Abilities*—organize knowledge into a coherent structure, revealing key relationships
3. *Questioning Abilities*—doubting or disputing to inquire or subject a message to more subtle analysis, checking things out
4. *Reasoning Abilities* — the ability to draw conclusions from data
5. *Linguistic Abilities*—language skills such as vocabulary, syntax, and rhetorical skills

Many individuals do not bring their intellectual abilities to bear when processing a text. Teachers are responsible for encouraging the thinking displayed through these attributes so that individuals can develop them for later independent use. Without viewing literacy as an intellectual transaction, individuals will be subject to the manipulation of the author's words. Finally, the last component of the model is the attribute of knowledge and experience. This is the sum of what an individual comprehends about the general knowledge of a topic and processing ability. These attributes are defined as follows:

1. *General Knowledge of a Topic*—organization of direct or indirect experiences
2. *Processing Ability*—the ability to extract, interpret and evaluate information and ideas from the text

These two aspects of this final component are most teachable and, therefore, a responsibility teachers face in developing habits of evaluative literacy.

These attributes must be developed because they may work interactively when processing text. This is so because some texts place more of a burden on one attribute rather than another. This means there is always an interplay of these attributes during processing.

What this model of the evaluative individual tells us is that achieving literacy, as we discussed earlier, means much more than simply taking a text at face value. To do so is not to think about the author's implicit message or point of view much. We must constantly be aware of how these attributes interact during the language–thought transaction of evaluative literacy. To do less is not to complete the instruction we aim to provide.

Next, we turn to a model that represents the processing of integrating evaluation with the ongoing comprehension process. We call it the Two-Tier Model of Comprehension and Evaluation (figure 1.4). It is drawn from work by Dagostino (1991) and Dagostino and Carifio (1994).

Evaluation Is Integral to Comprehension

Contrary to the predominant hierarchical view where evaluation occurs at the end of the comprehension process, the Two-Tier Model proposes that evaluation is an ongoing processing of text throughout all aspects of comprehending text (Dagostino, 1991; Dagostino & Carifio, 1994c; Dagostino et al., 2013, 2014). The Two-Tier Model rests on the following propositions:

1. The process of evaluation is interwoven with comprehension and interpretation.
2. Evaluation operates constantly throughout the individual–text interaction once an individual intends to do more than establish the literal sense of the text.
3. The nature of evaluation varies on at least three dimensions:

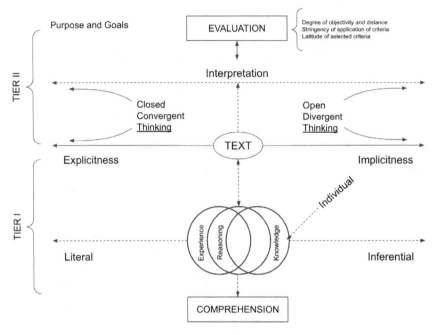

Figure 1.4   **The Two-Tier Model of Comprehension and Evaluation of Messages.**

    1. degree of objectivity and distance established
    2. stringency of the application of the criteria
    3. latitude of selected criteria
  4. This model partially counters a strict, sequential, hierarchical view of comprehension without compromising a component of analysis.
  5. Tier I and Tier II are interactive and progressive in nature. They are vertically and horizontally interactive.
  6. Both Tier I and Tier II are dependent upon the individual's background, albeit different aspects of background.
  7. An individual's background interacts with the text of varying degrees of explicitness along a continuum of literal to inferential comprehension.
  8. Closed, convergent thinking balances open, divergent thinking in a direct relationship with the explicit/implicit dimension of text and related interpretation.

    This model is organized around the principle that the process of evaluation, and perhaps that of appreciation, is interwoven with comprehension and constantly used throughout the individual–text interaction. This idea partially contrasts with a strict, sequential, hierarchical view of comprehension that suggests a direct progression from literal to inferential and then to evaluation, followed by appreciation and application in a step-like levels depiction of comprehension and evaluation.

The model represents a synthesis of interaction and hierarchy in the two tiers depicted in figure 1.4.

Several key terms are presented here before looking at how these components relate to each other in the proposed model.

Key Terms:

Tier II:

Evaluation:

Evaluation of a text is an individual's response to what they comprehend and represents their interpretation of the text's message. The expectations for a text may influence an individual's response, and in turn, the individual's expectations may bias interpretation and evaluation. Conversely, interpretation may influence evaluation. There seems to be a dynamic, reciprocal nature to these processes. The individual's evaluation of a text also may vary with:

the degree of objectivity and distance maintained;
the stringency of application of criteria;
the latitude of selected criteria.

Interpretation:

Interpretation of a text is an intermediate response in the process of evaluation to what an individual is comprehending in a text. Interpretation of the text may take at least two directions. First, when there is a mix of explicitness of text and closed convergent thinking, interpretation becomes close, text-bound, and perhaps even literal. Second, a mix of implicitness of text and open, divergent thinking may lead to multiple interpretations that are almost speculative. The nature of thinking takes two forms as follows:

Closed, Convergent Thinking:

A system of processing text which limits the direction the individual takes in drawing conclusions. This pattern of thinking usually leads the individual to a logical, focused, and limited set of conclusions or predictions about the meaning, interpretation, and evaluation of the text. Closed suggests an individual's expectations and specified criteria may influence thinking in a systematic manner.

Open, Divergent Thinking:

A system of processing text which multiplies the directions the individual takes in drawing conclusions, or establishing explanations and interpretations of a text. Open and divergent suggest the possibility of other than logical reasoning or structuring of the details in developing a synthesis of information or ideas. Interpretation may be other than generally expected and perhaps more creative. Creative is a novel structuring of information or a novel explanation of events. Internally consistent but logically unexpected.

Pivotal Point between the Two Tiers:

Text:

Text represents the author's message through degrees of explicitness/ implicitness. The degree of explicit/implicit nature of the text influences how the individual comprehends and interprets the message of the text.

Tier I:

Comprehension:

The process of comprehension by the individual moves along a continuum of literal to inferential in a manner similar to the explicitness or implicitness of the text's message. What the individual makes of text at this level is influenced by the individual and also provides the base for interpretation and evaluation. If text elements are not apprehended, they may not be filtered or included in either the open, divergent thinking or the closed, convergent thinking of interpretation. In turn, an evaluation fluctuates because some of the information was not processed.

Individual:

The experience with processing text, in general, or with a specific text/style/ form, combined with the individual's knowledge of the topic and ability to reason appropriately for the text, varied with each individual and across individuals. This trio of characteristics, experience, reasoning, and knowledge influences where the individual enters the literal-inferential scale of comprehension.

The Two-Tier Model: Relationships of the Components

With reference to figure 1.4, we can think of Tier I and Tier II as horizontally shifting plates that can move as a slide rule moves that are physically separate but related numerically and functionally.

Tier I covers the territory of comprehension from literal understanding and recall to inferential processes based on direct experience, general and specific knowledge, and reasoning.Although never completely separate from individuals' backgrounds, Tier I is more closely related to the cues in the text, which carry the message and shape the presentation as developed by the author to be apprehended by the individual.

The trio of circles represents the individual. Primarily, the trio represents the interaction of reasoning, experience, and knowledge as the interaction influences comprehension, interpretation, and evaluation.

Tier II draws upon and acts upon Tier I. That is, it relies heavily upon the individual's information and thinking, yet, it is still dependent upon the text message and how the individual creates and shapes their interpretation of the text.

Each tier has different goals. Tier I's goal is to depict getting the message and its clearly implied conclusions. Tier II's goal is to depict evaluating, with specified criteria, the message of Tier I. Tier II is the response part of the model where the response may be personal, subjective, or criteria objective given the individual's purpose and the criticalness of the judgments.

When we look carefully at the individual in relationship to the process depicted here, we see the individual's ability to evaluate shift dramatically depending upon the subject matter or the form of the text. The hope is that the mature individual will develop sufficient skill to raise general evaluative questions so that at least some sense of the text's veracity can be determined, regardless of the subject.

However, this model implies that as the individual's knowledge base and thinking skills equal or surpass that of the text, evaluation with specific criteria operates constantly so that the criteria don't come into play only after inferences are made; they operate while the individual selectively and judiciously chooses and evaluates what is stated directly and implicitly derived from the text. This means that evaluation also may shape interpretation.

A shifting horizontally of the Tier I and Tier II plates depict the uneven, dynamic nature of the comprehension-evaluation interaction. As the individual has different purposes and goals in mind, they may elect a different set of criteria for evaluation and, depending upon the criticalness of the decision, that is what is at stake, and apply the criteria stringently or leniently.

Interpretation plays an important part in this model because it is here we see evaluation shaping comprehension. Here the individual's background selects relevant details for their purpose and constructs a whole- or the meaning of the text. This meaning or interpretation may or may not be justifiable in light of the text's consistency of structure or the author's intent; however, it is this meaning derived from the text that the individual responds to evaluatively and appreciatively.

Johnson (1967) identifies three levels of experience that may be relevant here. The first level is at a basic literal/inferential level where there is acceptance of the message. The second level is a bit more critical, where there may be questioning and rejecting of the message. The third level is more creative, where there may be reshaping and restructuring of the message.

Each level represents varying degrees of interaction between the individual and the text. The interaction moves along a continuum of increasing dialogue and individual control of the text. Moving along the continuum, individuals become more active and evaluative in questioning the text and creating "text against text" to represent varying points of view. Text is negotiable because evaluation and reflection make comprehension dynamic.

In the first level of experience, there is a predictable expectation that may be passive and conventional. If a text does not follow the pattern of expectations, the individual becomes alert to the variation and the need to move to the second level of experience. In this second level of experience, there is an alternative view presented; this view is less conventional, less predictable, and more questioning of the "deferred reality." It is now a text of equivocation, one that forces a search for meaning as well as in-depth interpretation.

This level of experience forces a consideration of a counter-argument, which may lead to thinking about further alternatives. This kind of thinking leads to the third level of experience, which entails trying to synthesize the many semantic forces at play and comprehend the complex dynamics of their contradictions, equivocations, or pragmatics of the words and the ideas represented symbolically.

Individuals must become aware of themselves as individuals so they don't simply accept the text as in the first level of experience. For individuals to achieve all three levels of experience, they must cultivate an intellectual style that prompts them to be self-conscious about the assumptions and the goals of their processing and to process deliberately from a different perspective. Perhaps one individual follows the principles of logic, and one follows the aesthetics of language and themes.

When both templates are "working" simultaneously, the individual can respond to thought, structure, and style simultaneously and evaluate if the language is used effectively to carry the thinking and the emotion of the writer. Thus, both evaluation and appreciation are central to evaluative literacy as it relates to a variety of environments. This part of the text brings to a close a deep look at evaluative literacy that permeates the remaining chapters of this book.

CHAPTER SUMMARY

Chapter 1 has given us a historical progression through five periods of an evolving concept of literacy. We have accomplished this goal by following the progression and changes through time and identifying specific characteristics for evaluating text of all kinds. We have a good sense of the evaluative individual and the interactive evaluation process of text from the Model of the Attributes of the Evaluative Individual and the Two-Tier Model of Evaluation and Comprehension. Understanding this evolution should give you a context for further chapters.

Chapter 2

Moving into the Digital World

OVERVIEW

This chapter gives us a picture of the historical perspectives of media literacy, much as we did for literacy in Chapter 1. Here, we give some changes in theoretical views that reflect the contrast between traditional and digital text communication and the implications for present communication and visions for the future. We describe specific forms of media and why and how these forms influence the evaluation of messages. We look at how the ability to evaluate messages becomes more of a responsibility of the receiver of those messages than it was in the past.

GUIDING QUESTIONS

In what ways have the concepts of communication and media evolved?

How can content processing, structure, and patterns be described within all venues? Is there a shift from linear, continuous text to truncated, recursive text?

How do the five entities of (1) devices and venues, (2) navigation through each device, (3) processing of the text by the user, (4) language and text structure, and (5) types of media such as graphics, video, animation, and interactive influence the differences between traditional communication and digital communication?

How can we distinguish between the intended audience and users of devices and venues? Does it matter?

Who are the gatekeepers of all forms of communication?

What are the ethical concerns of communication?

What impact do the concepts such as influence and bias have on communication?

THE EVOLUTION OF THE CONCEPTS OF
COMMUNICATION AND MEDIA

Chapter 1 introduced you to part of the conceptual framework for this book by presenting the evolution and concept of literacy, specifically that of evaluation. This chapter parallels that work by focusing on media literacy and how the digital revolution influences our thinking on literacy as we move forward in time.

Understanding how this thinking will reflect the concept of literacy is crucial to setting standards for literacy instruction, assessment, and the nature of literacy proficiency for the future. So, we move into Chapter 2 to present the emerging concerns in this broadened view of literacy.

Distinguishing Communication and Media

Communication as a practice is as old as the first cave drawings and oral language of prehistoric peoples. As humans became more intentional about their communication, it evolved into a social concept. We often think of communication in various ways—oral, written, and, these days, electronic and digital transmissions. However, it is essential to distinguish between communication and media, as many people conflate the two. Communication is a message transmitted via a medium (book, television, radio, social media, etc.). The word media, in this sense, merely refers to more than one kind of medium. Like the evolution of literacy, media has a historical perspective, as noted here:

Stages of Media Evolution

There have been five stages in the evolution of media as a means of communication:

1. Oral Era (Pre to 1500 BCE): During this time, messages were passed through the spoken word.
2. Written Era (1500 BCE–1449 CE): As written language was developed, it quickly overtook oral traditions among certain groups of people. However, this skill was limited to those with money and power, often the ruling class within a society.
3. Print Era (1450–1843 CE): With Gutenberg's invention of the printing press in 1440 CE, we see the beginnings of the democratization of media. Literacy and communication were no longer the tools of the ruling class. During this time, we see significant upheavals in power dynamics and the beginnings of mass media. (Gutenberg was not the

first to develop a movable type press—this was done centuries earlier in China—but his invention was made of metal and included features that made the process easier and more economical.)

4. Electronic Era (1844–1980 CE): With the invention of media such as the telegraph, the radio, film, and television, mass communication became the primary mode of message transmission in the United States. Messages were instantaneous and could be spread to large groups at one time.

5. Digital Era (1980 CE to present): As digital media and the Internet have taken hold, communication has become even more prolific.

These stages of media evolution, like the five periods of literacy presented in Chapter 1, have influenced the evolving concept of literacy and the demand on individuals concerning good communication and the need for more evaluative processing of texts. The following theoretical models show the importance of recursiveness and feedback to the processing.

Theoretical Communication: Berlo, McLuhan, and Barland

Through the electronic age, three individuals have made important contributions to the evolution of media theory. They are Berlo, McLuhan, and Barland.

In 1960, communication theorist David Berlo created the SMCR Model of Communication (figure 2.1), which delineated the basic components of message transmissions: Source, Message, Channel, and Receiver. In this simplistic model, there is a source (person) who creates a message. They then choose the channel for that message (oral, written, electronic—more specific examples are a speech, newspaper column, television advertisement, etc.). Once transmitted, that message is received by an audience—perhaps an individual or a larger group.

One of the many critiques of Berlo's linear model is that it doesn't leave room for the distortion of the message, nor does it include the opportunity for the receiver to provide feedback to the source. It focuses on a linear transmission that ignores the recursive nature of most communication. However, given the time period in which he created this model, that is no surprise. Mass Media was the dominant form of communication in the 1960s, where a small

Figure 2.1   SMCR Model of Communication.

group of people had the power to send messages to the larger society. Aside from television ratings and letters to the editor, there were not many ways for the receiver to provide feedback to the sender.

Around the same time as Berlo developed his model of communication, media theorist Marshall McLuhan recognized the impact the choice of medium has on the message itself. He placed such a heavy emphasis on the medium's power that he coined the phrase, "The medium is the message" (McLuhan, 1964).

An easy way to see this applied is the difference between a newspaper article and a television news report. A newspaper article offers in-depth information, and the reader can take their time reviewing the words and rereading them as necessary. A television news report often gives only an overview of a news story accompanied by video and sound. Both messages need to be crafted with the strengths and norms of each media.

With the critique of Berlo and the insights of Berlo and McLuhan in mind, another model emerged. In 1970, Dean Barnlund developed the Transactional Model of Communication, which adds several important components to the SMCR Model, including a feedback loop. Barnlund recognized the transactional nature of communication, where both sender and receiver can influence the message through verbal, nonverbal, and behavioral cues.

He also emphasized the context of communication and its effects on the message. This includes societal norms, cultural identities, and the relationship between the sender and receiver. The Transactional Model of Communication also underscores the effect of noise—in other words, how external factors can influence or interrupt the flow of communication from Sender to Receiver.

Figure 2.2 is a visual representation of Barnlund's Model (TMOC). It seems more relevant as we move into the digital age. There are several components to the model, including:

Person: Can be either the sender or the receiver of a message.
Decoding: This occurs when the receiver assigns meaning to the verbal and nonverbal cues and the message.
Encoding: The process of communicating a message through verbal and nonverbal means.
Public Cues: Environmental cues occur outside of the communication process and can include natural and human-made elements.
Private Cues: These are cues that are relegated to the individual and their experiences and observations of text, photos, etc., as well as the personal feelings and emotions of the individual.
Nonverbal Behavioral Cues: Behaviors that communicate information; for example, posture, hand gestures, etc.
Behavioral Verbal Cues: These are spoken words used to communicate a message.
Message: A purposeful verbal or written communication.

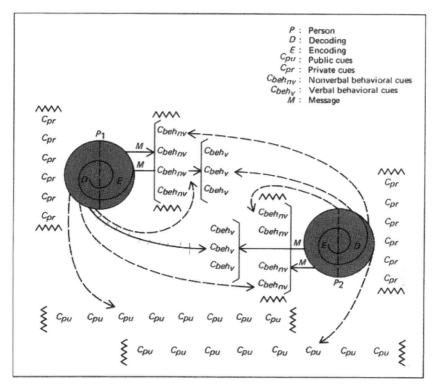

Figure 2.2 Barnlund's Transactional Model of Communication. Barnlund's Transactional Model, 1970 (Mortesen, 1972).

As humans communicate, there is a circular, transactional process of encoding and decoding messages. Each individual uses public, private, nonverbal behavioral, and behavioral verbal cues to encode and decode messages. Thus making Barnlund's Model more useful for the digital age. These characteristics influence the content and structure of texts as we progress into the digital age.

Progression into the Digital Age

As we have progressed from the electronic age (telephone, radio, television, and other analog media powered by electricity) to the digital age (computers, the Internet, social media, and other digital media), the power and opportunity to be the message source have spread to anyone with access to a smartphone or computer, and feedback opportunities have grown tremendously.

Think of social media, where anyone can comment on a Facebook post or respond to a TikTok. The number of likes a photo on Instagram receives is immediate feedback to the source. In this way, the evolution of media has directly affected communication. When applying these theories to new media, in particular, Barnlund's Model makes more sense. In addition to a feedback loop, interaction becomes an integral part of the communication process.

The Role and Effect of Intentionality

The intentionality of communication evolved as humans became more aware of the power of their words. Think back to the Ancient Greeks and philosophers like Aristotle, who developed the rhetorical theory that undergirds much of today's persuasive communication theory and technique in the United States. We see his theory in the messages of advertising, documentary films, social media, and so many more media.

Modern researchers, such as Anastasia Schmidt (2014), Farida Yasmin Panwar (2020), and Juyoung Song (2019), have explored other aspects of communication, such as how the sender modifies the message and/or chooses the channel based on the receiver. One excellent example of this is code-switching. This concept originated as a sociolinguistic theory wherein multilingual people moved between languages while speaking. However, this theory has been expanded to recognize the code-switching employed by monolingusitic people as they move between different dialects of their language. For example, Black people in the United States who speak AAVE (African American Vernacular English) will often change their grammar and vocabulary when speaking with white people.

The digital age brought greater recursiveness in the presentation and process of messages. A look at this processing will help us see the similarities and changes, all of which contribute to a greater evaluation of messages.

THE PROCESSING OF MESSAGE CONTENT AND STRUCTURE IN TRADITIONAL, ELECTRONIC, AND DIGITAL FORMS OF COMMUNICATION MEDIA

Print, Electronic, and Digital forms of communication media, while different, share many structures and patterns that allow consumers to require evaluative skills across platforms. A look at different forms will be helpful here to understand these variations. One thing to keep in mind is regardless of the medium, it is always important to consider who created the message and evaluate both what is included in the message and what is left out. For instance, whose voices are included, whose are excluded, what photographs are used, which are left out, what video and audio are included, and what is edited.

Traditional Print Forms of Communication Media

The text of traditional print media, such as books, magazines, and newspapers, have linear processing – words are read left to right and top to bottom. We learn this from our earliest experiences with literacy and continue to apply this practice as we are introduced to different forms of print media. Readers gain context and information as they move through the story or article.

In addition to text, traditional print media can include other forms of media, such as photographs and graphics. These visual elements provide additional information and context clues for the reader. Much like text processing, we learn how to evaluate these media through implicit and explicit instruction. However, the depth of these evaluative skills tends to be superficial and limited.

Electronic Communication Media

The invention of the electric telegraph in the mid-1800s ushered in a new means of communication. Telephones quickly followed, then radio, film, and finally, television. Unlike traditional print media, these new means of communication included live audio and video and required different evaluative skills. When listening to the audio, in addition to the verbal message, one needs to evaluate volume, pacing, and added aural information such as music or sound effects.

Film/video/television almost always includes audio, and when it does, the skills needed for aural evaluation are applied. When evaluating video, the evaluative process is similar to those used for still images, but it must also consider that it is a time-based medium. Regardless of the nature of the message (news, documentary, or narrative), one must consider not only the audio/video that is included but also what is left out of the frame or on the cutting room floor. A shift to digital communication required changes to the processing of messages.

DIGITAL COMMUNICATION MEDIA

There is often some confusion over the difference between electronic and digital media, particularly since television, radio, and film have evolved into digital mediums. These mediums exist in electronic (analog) and digital methods, though digital prevails these days.

Digital communication media extends to new media, including web pages and social media. These differ from the electronic forms of television, radio, and film in that they allow for a more transactional communication between the sender and receiver. The shifting toward digital forms of communication has brought challenges.

One major shift in the pattern of reading is the need to develop skills in lateral reading. Developing this skill is crucial for navigating digital forms of text.

LATERAL READING

Reading via web browser has presented both challenges and opportunities. While learning to navigate websites takes time, once students understand the landscape of web pages, they can use the platform to their advantage through "Lateral Reading." Lateral readers deeply analyze the information they find online. While reading a news article or text, they open multiple browser tabs to confirm the information in the original reading, research the author and publisher, and extend their understanding of the material:

> Lateral readers gain a better understanding as to whether to trust the facts and analysis presented to them. . . . Lateral reading helps the reader understand both the perspective from which the site's analyses come and if the site has an editorial process or expert reputation that would allow one to accept the truth of a site's fact. (Caulfield, 2017)

Again it heightens the need for navigational skills and analytical, evaluative reading, along with synthesizing a myriad of information. These skills present challenges to processing messages.

CHALLENGES RELATED TO ELECTRONIC AND DIGITAL FORMS OF COMMUNICATION MEDIA

However, despite the many similarities, Electronic and Digital communication presents different challenges than print media. Devices and venues such as computers, phones, social media, streaming video, digital, or audio require navigational and processing skills that are device and media-specific. Furthermore, there are additional processing and evaluative skills needed for graphics, video, audio, animated, and interactive media. A description of each media can suggest the skills needed.

Graphics

Graphics are hand-drawn images or images created using digital design tools and software. They include graphs, charts, and data plots. Books can have graphics in grayscale or color. In most newspapers, graphics are published in half-tone, which allows for shades of gray. It is usually on the front page of a newspaper that you find any color graphics.

Video

Video includes live-action television, film, and streaming media. It is almost always accompanied by audio and graphics and occasionally includes animation. (Technically, film and video are different mediums; however, in this digital age, they are both almost always captured as digital information rather than as analog media.)

Audio

We most often hear audio in conjunction with video; however, there are times it is isolated, such as on the telephone, radio, or as standalone audio clips on a website.

Animation

Animation is merely a graphic in motion. When we think of the origins of animation, we often picture hand-drawn cartoons. However, animation was born during the early experiments with photography and filmmaking. The kineograph, more commonly known as the flip book, was created by John Barnes Linnett in 1868. The principle works similarly to film in that a series of still images are shown in rapid succession, creating the appearance of movement. Our eyes connect the still images together in a phenomenon known as the persistence of vision. Over time, this process has evolved, and most animations are now digital creations.

Interactive Media

Interactive media allows the user to control their experience, at least to some degree. Think back to the "Choose your own adventure" books of the 1980s. These books allowed readers to pick from different options several times during the story. These days, interactive media tends to be digital and is commonly seen as a facet of social media and video games.

Returning to Chapter 1, we identified evaluative skills necessary for evaluating electronic and digital media. We will address them here with further discussion.

- Processing Different Kinds of Material Evaluatively
- Detecting Deception
- Seeking Credibility and Validity
- Developing Sensitivity to Language
- Algorithms

Processing Different Kinds of Material Evaluatively

Recognizing Conventions of Media

As we covered in Chapter 1, working with traditional print media entails understanding how the evaluation process is transformed for poetry, narrative, exposition, and argumentation by using specific criteria for formal evaluation. In addition to considering the genre of print media, we must also consider the media format (book, magazine, newspaper, etc.) As we learn how to process and evaluate text, we also learn the conventions of each media format. The same holds for electronic and digital text—we need to learn the conventions of each medium.

Although the conventions of print media, particularly books, are made explicit as part of the elementary school curriculum, students learn the conventions of many other media outside of the classroom—through exposure and use over time.

Take television as an example—most students do not explicitly learn about the conventions of television shows, commercials, public service announcements, etc. Still, through repeated exposure during childhood, they understand the function and nature of these kinds of television programming. The same holds for radio, websites, blogs, etc. Even though some of these media are text-based or text-heavy, they do not follow the same conventions of traditional books. One way is that there is a change in the formatting of text material.

Variations in Formatting of Grid Patterns

All forms of text media use a grid pattern to provide an underlying structure to the design. The most basic is a single-column grid—often called a manuscript grid. This is what we see with books. Multi-column grids lay out newspapers and magazines, while modular grids provide website structure. These grids allow for the expansion and truncation of text areas relative to the size of the browser or screen used to view the media.

Whereas books are generally formatted with text that is the same font and size, newspapers and magazines use visual hierarchy to lead their reader through a story. We can see a visual hierarchy through headlines, subheadings, and chunking text. As we develop our evaluative skills, we understand that the largest text is reserved for the most essential information, and the smallest text is the least important information. We also see visual hierarchy in the placement of photographs and graphics.

Additionally, newspapers and magazines are often written using an inverted-pyramid style, providing the reader with the essential information in the first paragraph or two of the story. The expectation is that readers will often skim over articles. Therefore, the most important information needs to be at the beginning of the article, and the user can continue reading if they want further detail and context.

Websites often integrate traditional reading patterns into their design. Returning to the idea that English readers move their eyes left to right and top to bottom, many websites are designed to take advantage of this habit. For example, the main logo is placed in the top left of the design, with the main menu bringing the eye from left to right across the page. The eye then moves back to the left and crosses the page in an almost Z-pattern—often called a Gutenberg Diagram (figure 2.3). The termination point is the bottom right corner of the page, where a call to action is often placed.

One way websites differ from traditional print documents is that they are often based on a fluid design. In other words, as the web browser is enlarged or shrunk, the website expands or contracts with it. This design allows users more control over text size and accompanying graphics and photographs.

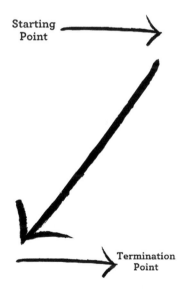

Starting Point

Termination Point

Figure 2.3   Gutenberg Diagram.

It also means that designs will look the same (or virtually the same) on various digital devices, including smartphones, tablets, computers, etc. These changes require evaluation in processing media.

Learning to Evaluate Media

Elementary students generally do not receive explicit instruction on how to process and evaluate multimedia and online text. Some middle schools are incorporating "digital literacy" classes into their curriculum; however, most students enter high school and college lacking the necessary skill and foundational knowledge for deep analysis and evaluation. Furthermore, this kind of evaluation is twofold – students need the skills to evaluate both the content of the media and the form in which it is presented.

As noted earlier, theorist Marshall McLuhan wrote extensively about the power of media to transform the message. It requires explicit instruction to learn how to separate a message from its media and to understand and evaluate how specific media influences one's perception of a message.

When it comes to new media in particular, applying these evaluative skills requires a more nuanced understanding of the relationship between media and their messages. These following skills are often applied to traditional print media evaluation; however, in today's digital age, they are more critical than ever. Students will face a barrage of confusing, conflicting, and fabricated messages from various new media.

To wade through the junk to find accurate, factual information, they need both technical and evaluative skills. (Lateral reading, as described earlier, is one of the foundational skills they need as they learn to navigate the web of digital media.)

Detecting Deception

As noted in Chapter 1, detecting deception focuses on recognizing propaganda and whether it sells something or someone of value. When the purpose is to persuade, the individual must recognize the writer's slant of information and ideas. The individual must recognize the situational purpose of a text and weigh the message and the presentation.

Electronic and digital forms of communication media, coupled with the vast amount of information available, make it incredibly difficult to identify misinformation and disinformation without explicit instruction and well-developed evaluative skills. There is a proliferation of both misinformation and disinformation in today's media. While misinformation and disinformation are both forms of false information that are created and spread (often through social media), only disinformation is created with the intent to deceive.

Detecting deception is a crucial evaluative skill when determining the validity of information and distinguishing between misinformation and disinformation. This is even more complex when electronic and digital media are used to spread information. Video, audio, and photographs tend to elicit more profound emotional responses than just text alone. Merely adding music to a message can change the very nature of how it is perceived. Think of watching a horror film – if you turn off the sound (and the scary music that is included), the fear dissipates.

Unfortunately, news from traditionally credible sources, such as newspapers and television, can be riddled with misinformation. Almost all news outlets have websites and use social media platforms to expand their reach. This is because of the need to stay relevant and compete with digital news sources. News and information spread quickly through platforms like Facebook, Twitter, and TikTok, leaving traditional news outlets scrambling to compete. Their haste to be the first to break a news story has led to a rise in misinformation.

In today's environment of social media, citizen journalism, and "fake news," media literacy has become an essential skill for media consumers. But how do we know what is reliable and credible? Unfortunately, with the advent of the Internet and Social Media, anyone can publish "news," which has led to a rise in bogus websites, "Fake News," doctored videos, and more.

What is Fake News? First of all, "Fake News" is a made-up term widely propagated by former President Trump. There is no such thing as "Fake News." It does not mean news that you don't like or shows you in a negative light. There is news, and there is deliberate misinformation or a hoax spread with the intent of misleading people——disinformation. This is usually done for financial or political gain. Any form of media can spread this kind of deceptive information. This is why students need to develop the skills to identify the credibility and validity of both information and its source.

Seeking Credibility and Validity

As mentioned in Chapter 1, Seeking Credibility and Validity, processing evaluatively focuses on distinguishing Fantasy from Reality or Fact from Opinion based on authenticity, adequacy, and relevance, as well as logic and argument. It entails recognizing the influence of beliefs and attitudes that are part of a person's moral structures and knowing what to believe or to do. Doing this means determining the truth unbiased by moral views of an issue. Individuals are looking for plausibility and possibility of the occurrence of events and internal validity.

When seeking credibility and validity, one thing to remember is that anyone can publish on the Internet. No ethical codes or standards compel the average person to share credible information. There are many fact-checking sites available to help you determine fact from fiction. The following are examples of these sites:

- FactCheck.org
- Politifact.com
- Snopes.com

However, although there are plenty of resources to help one identify mis- and disinformation, it's critical that students learn to develop the evaluative skills they need to sort through the piles of information they encounter daily.

The first step is to examine the news source and author. Is the information being communicated by an established news outlet? Or is it an independent source, such as a blogger or citizen journalist? Always check if there is an "about us" page if it is a website or a link to a bio if it is on social media. Second, examine the source for any bias. Inevitably, there will be evidence of bias. Professional news sources will ameliorate bias with transparency, but most sources will not acknowledge their biases.

When first learning to detect bias online, you can use tools to help you confirm or debunk your analysis. Here's a great site that allows you to enter a news media source and find out its bias rating, whether it leans toward one side of the political spectrum, and its track record regarding sourcing and transparency—Media Bias Fact Check (http://mediabiasfactcheck.com). You can also use the Allsides Media Bias Chart (https://www.allsides.com/media-bias/media-bias-chart) and the Media Bias Chart (https://adfontesmedia.com/) from ad fontes for quick reference when identifying the credibility and depth of major news outlets.

Detecting bias on the web can be difficult because anyone can post a website or create a blog. Traditional news sources, such as television and radio, are overseen by the FCC and ethical associations and codes for their respective industries. However, social media and blogging tools are not beholden to these regulations or ethical standards. Anyone can make a "news" website and post disinformation. There are no consequences for such an action, and it can quickly have a domino effect as social media users share articles from that site, spreading the lies far and wide.

Opportunity for Interactions

With traditional print media, there is rarely an opportunity to interact with the author outside of a letter to the editor or author. These interactions fall very much under the antiquated theories of communication like S-M-C-R. However, social media and web-based media allow both asynchronous and synchronous interaction between media makers and media consumers in the form of discussion boards, social media posts (tweets, TikTok videos, etc.), and reader comments. During the print era, journalists were not expected to engage directly with their audience as they do now. Writers are often expected to respond to readers' comments online and maintain a social media presence.

Beyond journalism media, social media has become an interactive source of news and information. Citizen journalists have usurped traditional journalists in many breaking news stories, using their smartphones to broadcast live and breaking news on the spot. Additionally, social media allows for the transmission of information at an unprecedented rate. Twitter, in particular, lends itself to breaking news. For example, the Hudson River Plane crash was tweeted live by a witness to the plane landing in the Hudson.

This rise in social media as a news source has drawn readers away from traditional print media sources. According to the latest research from the Pew Research Center, roughly 50 percent of Americans get their news from social media sources (2022). Facebook is the most used site for news consumption. Around 70 percent of Americans use Facebook, and 31 percent of them, get their news from the social media giant.

However, Facebook has the laxest ethical standards of all social media platforms. Rarely do they remove deceptive or fabricated "news," and their algorithms often leave users stuck in a filter bubble that only regurgitates news and information they already agree with. This poses a particular problem for those who have not had the opportunity to develop their news media literacy skills.

Developing Sensitivity to Language

As we wrote in Chapter 1, developing sensitivity to language focuses on diction, denotation and connotation, tone, figurative language, and use of syntax. Individuals must become sensitive to the framing of a message and the words chosen to create a particular tone. Additional features are formal or informal register, symbolic or abstract language, and the overall effect of phrasing and sentence structure.

The language of social media is unlike traditional print media in that it is truncated and often incorporates or relies solely on visual images such as photographs, graphics, videos, and animations. Further complicating matters, websites, social media, and apps can be accessed through various platforms, including computers (desktop and laptop), tablets, and smartphones. What information is presented and how it appears often depends on the device from which it is accessed. Most websites have mobile versions that appear when accessed via tablet or smartphone. Students need the skills to evaluate media messages sent through various platforms and devices.

Social media posts are almost always truncated. Services like Twitter limit users to 280 characters per "Tweet." Facebook encourages users to post videos or photos along with their written text and prioritizes posts with images over those without. This means that information is often reduced to either the most critical information or the information most likely to convince the viewer to click a link or article for more information. Often, this results in misleading headlines known as "clickbait."

Most everyone has fallen for clickbait at one time or another. The headline for an article is so compelling that you click on the link only to find the headline and/or associated picture has no connection to the information in the article. Clickbait is both frustrating and a form of deception. Media sources that rely on clickbait risk losing their credibility.

Another trap many folks fall for is loaded language—these are nonneutral terms for controversial or contested topics. Some examples would be using a term like "gay marriage" rather than "marriage equality," "pro-life" rather than "anti-abortion," "pro-choice" rather than "abortion rights advocate," and "illegal alien" rather than "undocumented immigrant." Loaded terms are imbued with preconceived notions, subconsciously prompting the audience toward a specific viewpoint.

Finally, the lack of formality of language on the web and social media greatly contrasts what is expected of printed newspapers, books, and magazines. The text on websites, like social media platforms, is often truncated. However, unlike print media, they have the added benefit of including hyperlinks to information and data. This allows users to dive deeper into the information they are learning. Media sources can provide more in-depth reporting and information sharing while keeping the primary article short and to the point.

Photos, videos, and animations further add to the complexity of the web. These are often embedded in online and social media messages. Photos and videos have historically added a layer of authenticity to news; however, with the rise in digital manipulation tools, we can no longer assume all photographs and videos are real and compelling proof. It is almost impossible to spot artificially generated videos or manipulated photos. One has to dig deep and consider the source, using the skills of seeking credibility and validity to evaluate visual media.

Learning to navigate the informal language of the web can be challenging, especially when you consider the addition of shorthand, such as emoticons and emojis. When computers as a means of communication were invented (think emails, instant messaging, etc.), the same issues existed as did with letters and telegraphs—text messages lacked context clues gathered from facial expressions and vocal tones. Not to mention, it was clunky to type long passages.

From these issues, emoticons & acronyms were born. Now you could let someone know you were LOL (laughing out loud) and even show them a smile. :o) Emoticons ☺ have become fancy emojis, allowing us to express our emotions in even greater detail. ☺ And now we have bitmojis that make it even more personal. It is not uncommon for people to respond online and on social media using these communication tools.

Algorithms

Algorithms are mathematical formulas used by search engines (such as Google) and social media platforms (such as Facebook, Instagram, Twitter, and TikTok) to tailor information for each user based on their social media habits and personal tastes. The major problem with algorithms is that they tend to create an echo chamber—users are only shown media with which the algorithms calculate they will most likely interact. This means that individuals tend only to see and hear information that conforms to their beliefs and values. This leads to confirmation bias, which reinforces one's beliefs and makes it less likely that one will be open to opposing views.

Getting stuck in a loop created by algorithms creates a "filter bubble." This makes it difficult to find information that challenges your beliefs and values. Without such a challenge, one cannot honestly evaluate the information they receive from media sources. There are ways to get out of your filter bubble, including:

- When searching the Internet, take the time to log out of your Google account. Otherwise, Google can track all of your searches and add them to their database of information about you. This will tailor all your search results to appeal to you as an individual.
- When googling, don't just look at the first few links; scroll down and check the next results page.
- Clear your search history, and be mindful of the cookies being used by websites and apps. Think of cookies as little trackers left behind that allow websites and apps to collect data points about you.
- Disable your location services on your phone—each app tracks your location and uses that information to tailor the ads and information they send to you.
- Clear your search history.
- Follow people and news sites that offer different opinions and perspectives than your own. That will help throw off the algorithm.
- Another great resource is to take the filter bubble quiz here: https://www .filterbubble.lu. This quiz will let you know how stuck you are and offer ideas for popping your filter bubble.

There is a common thread through these five evaluative skills—the need to identify and evaluate the media maker—the messenger. Where in times past, media would funnel through a few sources, nowadays, anyone can publish their work. This is a significant concern and change in overall communication within the transformation of the gatekeeping process. A look at how gatekeeping has changed is integral to the evaluative process.

GATEKEEPERS OF COMMUNICATION

The role of the gatekeeper in communication is to sift through information and choose what to share with a broader audience. This is a position of power, as the gatekeeper can influence public opinion and social norms. Gatekeeping as a concept was first coined by social psychologist Kurt Lewin in 1943, although he did not employ it as a means of describing communication. That came later in 1950 when journalism professor David Manning White studied how newspaper editors acted as gatekeepers when choosing which news stories to share with the larger public.

Although the term is relatively new, the practice of gatekeeping goes back to the birth of communication itself. During the oral era, the elders of a community would share the history of their group with the younger members. This tradition of storytelling became entrenched in cultures around the world and was often relegated to those who could tell stories well and could remember vast amounts of information. These folks were the first gatekeepers of communication – they transmitted messages to an audience.

As the media evolved, so did the role of gatekeeper. During the written era of communication, gatekeepers tended to be those with money and power. Often monks were tasked with writing religious texts, including copies of the Bible. Only the literate could communicate through written manuscripts. However, their influence was limited because of the time it took to create one book—the process was long and arduous, so their reach was limited.

Gutenberg's printing press revolutionized the role of the gatekeeper. Access to a printing press allowed one to communicate a message to a wide audience. However, the audience was still limited to those who were literate. Who was able to own and operate a printing press also limited the kinds of information that were disseminated. There was quite a bit of religious propaganda created in the early days of the printing press, and eventually, more scientific literature and newspapers were produced.

The electronic era brought with it an even more evolved concept of gatekeeper. This was the golden age of mass media, where a few companies owned the majority of media outlets. Radio producers decided what went on air, DJs chose the songs to play, film production companies chose the films to fund and produce, news agencies decided the stories to play on the nightly news, etc. Once again, those with money and power controlled the messages.

The digital age brought with it unprecedented democratization of communication. Though plenty of traditional gatekeepers remain, practically everyone with access to the Internet has the opportunity to communicate a message through their personal social media accounts. This shift has also come with a new concept called gatewatching, in which bloggers and other media users curate the stories and information published by major news outlets and government agencies. Citizen journalism, found on open sites like Wikinews and CNNiReport, allows people outside of the traditional news media paradigm to report on news and critique mainstream news coverage.

Additionally, the role of the audience has changed over time as feedback loops have been incorporated into digital media platforms. No longer relegated to just writing a letter to the editor, the average citizen can interact with journalists, authors, screenwriters, film producers, and more through social media apps like Twitter. They can also provide direct feedback and criticism via comments on websites. Where once the gatekeeper was a role limited to professionally trained journalists and those with the power and money to operate a media company, it is now open to anyone with access to the Internet. This ability raises the question of what is acceptable to communicate via these venues.

THE FIRST AMENDMENT AND FREEDOM OF SPEECH

The First Amendment is a fundamental part of the media in the United States. When the framers of the Constitution established the idea of a free press, it was modeled after the European phrase "The Fourth Estate." In this respect, the press is essentially a fourth branch of the government, providing a check on the other three branches: the Presidency, Congress, and the Supreme Court. These days, many folks invoke their "freedom of speech" as a defense for spreading mis- and disinformation. However, this is not the case. Freedom of Speech merely protects citizens from being censored by the government; it does not absolve them of the social and legal consequences of their actions.

As students learn about media literacy and their responsibilities as media consumers, they must understand how the First Amendment applies to media. This is particularly important as they inevitably will become media makers at some point. It is almost impossible to avoid this role in the social media landscape. Even an act as simple as posting a photo on Instagram transforms one's role from media consumer to media maker. This is why students need to understand the laws that protect them, as well as the ethical considerations needed to guide them as they become media producers and, essentially, media curators and gatekeepers.

ETHICAL CONCERNS IN TRADITIONAL, ELECTRONIC, AND DIGITAL FORMS OF COMMUNICATION MEDIA

The role of gatekeeping comes with myriad ethical considerations. During the late 1800s, newspapers often relied on sensationalized headlines and exaggerated reporting to attract readers. There were no ethical codes that dictated the behavior of editors, nor were there any consequences for breaking public trust. That changed in 1922 when the Atlantic Monthly magazine published articles criticizing the practices of the newspaper industry. Later that year, editors from several major newspapers formed the American Society of Newspaper Editors and developed a code of ethics.

Since that time, ASNE (The American Society of Newspaper Editors) has changed its name to the American Society of News Editors in 2009 to reflect the growing preponderance and influence of online news sources.

> Today, the American Society of News Editors is not just an organization for an elite tier of newsroom leaders. Its members are actively engaged in developing the next generation of leaders in digital journalism, championing First Amendment freedoms, and working to help U.S. news organizations become as vibrant and diverse as America is today. (ASNE, 2009)

Electronic communication media bring another level of ethical concerns that do not apply to print media. For example, television news viewers can be swayed by video and audio media. Dramatic and graphic images can make a powerful impact on the viewer. Music and sound effects can affect viewers at a visceral level. Viewers are drawn to audio/visual media, yet it often lacks in-depth reporting in newspapers and long-form journalism.

One of the reasons ethical behavior is so important in communication and media is because social media has allowed almost every person with Internet access to become a gatekeeper. With the click of a button, anyone can share information over social media. Because of this, users need to think before they post, or they run the risk of sharing misinformation.

And misinformation runs rampant on the web. In fact, "fake news" spreads faster and broader than credible, reputable news. A 2018 study by Vosoughi et al. examined tweets from 2007 to 2016. They found that "about 126,000 rumors were spread by ~3 million people. False news reached more people than the truth; the top 1% of false news cascades diffused to between 1000 and 100,000 people, whereas the truth rarely diffused to more than 1000 people" (p. 1146). A large part of this is because of the breakdown of the role of the gatekeeper. No longer does news and information funnel solely through ethical news organizations; because anyone can publish online, anyone can become a gatekeeper.

Another concern is the sharing of explicit or personal information. Without ethical standards or journalism training to guide gatekeepers, they are more likely to share offensive/harmful audio/visual media and commit an invasion of privacy. For example, employees of a company specializing in crime scene cleanup posted graphic photos of their work assignments on Facebook. Journalism training would have informed their decision, but without that ethical background, they broke very clear ethical standards.

All of what has been said in this chapter illustrates how our concerns about evaluation being central to literacy are essential in the digital world. They are at the heart of the impact of bias and influence on all types of communication. As we move forward in the next chapters, we hope to illustrate how our concerns influence our measures of literacy proficiency.

CHAPTER SUMMARY

This chapter shows how media reflects the evolving concept of literacy and how important it is that both the creator and the receiver of messages must be clear in the use of communication. The discussion in this chapter illustrates how what has been said about evaluation needs to be applied in the digital world. In this chapter, we also see how communication is transformed in the digital world and how we must adapt to it. Finally, following Chapter 1, this chapter prepares us for what we will say about integrating instruction, assessment, and professional development in subsequent chapters.

PART II

LITERACY PROFICIENCY

INSTRUCTION AND ASSESSMENT

Guiding Instruction

OVERVIEW

Chapter 3 focuses on concerns related to the instruction of evaluative literacy. It does so by examining the instructional environment and principles of instruction relative to traditional text and media. Sample lessons are given for the characteristics of evaluative literacy in the forms of communication discussed in this book. Similarities and differences in each of the forms of communication are addressed.

GUIDING QUESTIONS

What are the principles and applications for instruction for evaluative literacy for all forms of communication?

Are there variations and overlaps in the instruction of evaluative literacy between traditional text and media?

What are the affordances of technology in both types of communication?

What are some samples for the instruction of the characteristics of evaluative literacy that make applications of some of the principles of instruction?

In what ways does classroom learning differ from various types of digital learning?

Is social media a special form of digital communication requiring specific types of instruction?

SHIFTING TO LITERACY PROFICIENCY

Having presented a conceptualization of the evolving concept of literacy in a digital world, we move into characterizing literacy proficiency as reflected in instruction and assessment. The hope is that doing so takes ideas from Chapters 1 and 2 and shows their application in instructional practices and assessment measures. We do this by beginning with instructional concerns in Chapter 3 and then moving to ideas on assessment later in Chapter 4.

INSTRUCTIONAL ENVIRONMENT AND PRINCIPLES

When we consider factors contributing to effective instruction for evaluative literacy, we look to the instructional environment and principles for both traditional text and media. In doing so, we have identified four areas of concern: (1) classroom communities, (2) shared responsibilities, (3) paths for interaction, and (4) lesson structure and content. The discussion below considers each of these four factors for all instructional environments.

Classroom Communities

Creating classroom communities is at the heart of maximizing learning opportunities for all learners. When envisioning classroom communities, educators often think of learners signing behavior contracts, participating in establishing class rules, or working individually or in small groups in comfortable spaces in a well-designed classroom space. Yet, the vision of the classroom community is much more than what is easily visible. Classroom communities flourish when learners' voices are heard, learners' questions are encouraged, and learners' hearts are felt.

This vision of classroom community expands to include the qualities of rigor, inquiry, and intimacy, which are key to creating a culture and climate of thinking (Perkins, 1993).

Embedded in this belief of the classroom community as the cornerstone of learning is the understanding that building relationships, establishing trust, and creating working literate environments is crucial.

In *Life as a Crowded Place*, Ralph Peterson describes learning communities this way:

> Teachers who make communities have a big order to fill. . . . It is not unusual in today's classroom to find three, five, and sometimes more cultures represented. Bringing learners together and nurturing tolerance for their ways and beliefs while celebrating their differences challenges the talents of even the most experienced educators. . . . Teachers who make communities with their learners are cultural engineers of a sort. . . . Making meaning requires learners be responsible for their own learning, collaborate with others, and learn from their failures as well as successes. learners don't need to agree with one another, but they do need to see themselves as being responsible for others and find value in

group life. The educator takes the lead in making him or herself into a trusted person (p.13).

Classroom communities play a critical role in learning, and they have a special significance with regard to evaluative literacy. For learners to engage in the higher-level thinking skills involved in evaluative literacy: critical thinking, interpretive skills, and independent questioning. Learners need to be empowered through learning communities to have the confidence and skill to engage with texts in meaningful ways.

Through articulating their own ideas, listening to the ideas of others, clarifying and revising their own ideas, broadening their perspectives, and understanding the benefits of risk-taking, learners are engaging in the principles that guide evaluative literacy. This positive learning environment guides the educator in developing instruction in which the learners and educators share responsibility for learning.

Shared Responsibility

One model that serves as a framework to capture the balance and shifting of responsibilities inherent in the teaching/learning relationship is the Gradual Release of Responsibility Model (Pearson & Gallagher, 1983). The process of learning to ride a bicycle illustrates this model. The first step of learning to ride a bicycle often involves observing others riding bicycles. That initial step is often followed by actual attempts at riding a bike with help from a parent, older sibling, or an experienced friend. This help and accompanying feedback often provide the basis for the final step of independence.

Pearson and Gallagher's model of explicit reading instruction involves four stages:

1. Teacher modeling and explanation of strategy.
2. Guided practice, where teachers gradually give students more responsibility for task completion.
3. Independent practice accompanied by feedback.
4. Application of the strategy in real reading situations.

Teacher modeling is vital when educators are explaining evaluative literacy. As learners learn about evaluative literacy, educator modeling, and explicit explanation will help learners understand the processes which they are expected to use as they read.

Guided Practice involves scaffolding the task so that learners can practice the strategy with immediate feedback and support from the educator, and then as learners become more successful in applying the strategy, they can continue to practice the strategy more independently. This step embodies Vygotsky's belief in the zone of proximal development, which refers to the difference between what a learner can do without help and what he or she can achieve with the guidance and support of an educator or a skilled peer.

Independent Practice involves providing learners with time to practice a specific strategy and receive feedback from the educator. This practice and feedback allow learners to refine their understanding and application of the strategy. Application involves learners applying the strategy to a wide variety of reading materials. At this stage, learners are more flexible in their thinking and can understand connections among various strategies as well as better understand the ways that each strategy helps them understand the text more deeply. This is central to applying evaluative literacy strategies to a wide variety of texts.

The principles and practices that support the Gradual Release of Responsibility Model can be reflected in creating conditions for learning, such as providing learners with choices, a variety of materials for a broad range of responses, time, and a predictable structure.

PROVIDE LEARNERS WITH CHOICES

Learners should be allowed opportunities to make choices about their reading and writing. This refers not only to content but also to the form of the response (Cox & Many, 1992). Learners may respond to a literary work through a variety of forms: nonfiction pieces, poems, stories, plays, and essays, as well as social media platforms and other forms of digital text. Learners may also organize their responses in other modes, such as art or music. The opportunity to choose both materials and a way to respond is central to the learning process.

Provide Learners with a Wide Variety of Texts

Educators should provide children with a wide variety of texts. Many current educators repeatedly confirm the importance of providing learners with a wide variety of texts, such as nonfiction pieces, poems, stories, plays, essays, and graphic novels, as well as social media platforms and other forms of digital text (Atwell, 2009; Krashen, 2004; Keene & Zimmerman, 2007; Routman, 2002; Weaver, 2009).

Provide Learners with Time

Learners need time to explore ideas and feelings to arrive at new and deeper meanings. This belief that educators should provide learners with time to engage with texts of all sorts, both digital and traditional, and opportunities to respond is echoed in educational literature (Cox & Many, 1992; Krashen, 2004; Weaver, 2009).

Provide Learners with Opportunities to Talk

Educators should provide opportunities for learners to talk. Learners need time to reflect on their reading and writing, talk with each other, and discuss their reading and writing with their educators. This belief that discussion is necessary for a deeper understanding of the text is echoed in educational literature (Cazden, 2001; Goodman, 1986; Probst, 2004).

CREATE A TRUSTING ENVIRONMENT

Educators must strive to set up an atmosphere of trust, discussion, enthusiasm, and acceptance (Prest & Prest, 1988; Probst, 2004). Each of these authors stresses the importance of a positive classroom environment to create a feeling of security that allows learners to take the necessary risks to grapple with the complexities of all sorts of texts.

Evaluative literacy requires learners to question, explore, consider opposing viewpoints, and construct multiple perspectives to understand the meaning of the texts. Learners need a positive learning environment to engage in meaningful learning. Within this environment, a balance of classroom exchanges is critical to learning, and each day, several paths of interaction are available to learners and educators. This balance of shared responsibility is critical for learning.

Paths of Interaction

Four interaction paths often occur in the classroom, and each path contributes to learner learning. They are (1) whole-class instruction, (2) learning between pairs of learners, (3) small-group dynamics, and (4) individual independent learning. At the heart of each pathway is a commitment to teaching and learning through dialogue. Participating in dialogue contributes to learning and is essential for learners to become skilled in evaluative literacy.

Dialogue differs from a conversation in that informal conversation can veer off in many unexpected directions; through dialogue, learners and educators attempt to remain focused on understanding a specific topic. While engaging in dialogue, each group member must listen thoughtfully to the ideas expressed by other learners and respectfully offer his or her own ideas. Learners and educators engage in dialogue to deepen understanding, construct meaning, and critique ideas. While participating in dialogue, learners acquire the higher-level thinking skills that form evaluative literacy.

Two specific qualities are evident in dialogue and evaluative literacy— the ability to consider various ideas and to think critically about those ideas. Achieving evaluative literacy skills requires practice across various contexts, and each of the four pathways provides multiple opportunities for learners to acquire evaluative literacy skills through engaging in various forms of dialogue. The psychologist Vygotsky (1978) reminds us that by giving our learners practice in talking, we give them frames for thinking independently.

Whole-Class Instruction

This pathway of whole-class instruction provides educators with the opportunity to model strategies, explain concepts, make their inner thinking processes visible to learners, and observe their learners' understanding to inform instruction. Learners benefit from educator modeling of active listening, thoughtful responses, making inferences, understanding multiple viewpoints, and developing logical arguments.

In a whole-class setting, the educator is providing the critical step of showing learners how to find meaning in the task at hand. Whether the task is answering a question in history, writing a thesis statement, hypothesizing in science, problem-solving in math, or dealing with social behaviors, learners benefit when educators address the critical processes to work through each task. In this whole-class setting, the educator is providing learners with the tools to understand how to proceed, continue, and understand at deeper levels. By frequent modeling, the educator provides the necessary support for the learners to gradually assume the responsibility of becoming independent learners.

Different types of texts provide opportunities to teach different aspects of evaluative literacy. Through whole-class instruction, educators can focus on various aspects of evaluative literacy. For example, some texts are excellent models for understanding logic and developing strong arguments, other texts are exemplary examples of understanding inferences, and other texts serve to assist learners in understanding the point of view of others and the power of compassion and empathy. There are many interaction paths within whole-class instruction, and each path opens a door that leads to a stronger and more complete grasp of evaluative literacy.

Pairs of Learners

In this pathway of learners working in pairs, the balance of responsibility shifts to learners. In paired reading, learners read with a partner. When they need help or have a comment they would like to articulate, they have a partner with whom they can share. In this setting, learners can also practice the strategies the educator modeled in the whole group. For example, learners can practice working collaboratively by taking turns talking, asking questions, working together to answer questions, drawing inferences, and working together to understand the meaning of the text.

Working in pairs also provides learners with space for each of them to elaborate on each other's comments without the educator assuming the central role. To help learners think, talk, discuss, and write about texts, educators must provide time for them to explore texts. Partner reading provides time for learners to begin to share ideas with one another, discuss responses, and engage in critical thinking. When considering ways to help learners become engaged readers, writers, and learners, partner reading is one path in which the interactions can lead to excitement, enjoyment, and satisfaction when uncovering layers of meaning.

Working in pairs and then working in a small group helps learners to share multiple perspectives without being overwhelmed by the many varied perspectives of a large group.

Small-Group Dynamics

Guided Reading and Writing Groups

Oftentimes, in small groups, the guidance of the educator allows each learner to continue to improve as a reader and writer. Depending on what the educator observes in individual conferences, learners are brought together to work on a specific strategy. The goal is that learners will progress as they receive instruction designed for that specific strategy. The time period in which the group stays together depends on the learners' progress. Learners will move on from the group when they demonstrate an understanding of the strategy and the ability to apply it effectively. Learners continue to assume more responsibility for their learning as they improve in their reading and writing.

Book Clubs

Book Clubs, another type of small-group instruction, can be formed to provide learners with the opportunity to meet with their peers to discuss books. While there are varying formats for book clubs, one shared goal is for learners to engage in discussion and collaboration. Through discussion, learners can develop the confidence to express themselves and become empowered to think for themselves. Through discussion, learners also learn how to listen to the thoughts of another person.

As learners communicate and collaborate, their thinking deepens, and their perspective broadens. Learning experiences such as book clubs allow learners to engage in aspects of evaluative literacy, such as understanding multiple perspectives and interpretive thinking.

In both of these types of small groups, a rule of thumb is to limit the size of the group to four or five learners. One learner can assume the role of discussion leader, and another can be a recorder of the major points. This helps to manage the work and to bring the work to the large group for sharing and synthesizing ideas.

LEARNERS PRESENTING WORK TO WHOLE GROUP

It is critical to allow learners time to present their work to the whole class. What learners choose to share and celebrate may vary, but central to this process is shifting the responsibility to the learners. The topic may be a book talk or a book project such as an author or genre study. Learners may also share their writing of stories, poetry, and nonfiction. Perhaps they are sharing a letter they wrote to a former educator or grandparent, a petition they designed and created, a graphic novel, or a creative mix of graphics with words. Learners may share with their whole class, or they may visit another class to share.

Knowing they will have an audience to present their work helps learners assume responsibility and approach their work seriously. Learners come to anticipate this time as a time to share their voices. When learners are appreciated and valued for their work, their self-esteem is strengthened, and they are empowered to continue to deepen their thinking.

The questions and comments from their peers, as well as the critiques they receive, help them improve their evaluative literacy skills. As learners gain the confidence and skills to share and present with the whole class, they learn what it means to exchange ideas, change minds, hold fast to opinions while staying open to broadening perspectives, and listen and learn. When learners assume the role of sharing with the whole class, they are engaging in the core of evaluative literacy.

Independent Individual Learning

Here is where the responsibility for learning shifts from the educator to the learner. The modeling and explaining that occurred during whole-class instruction, the scaffolding of instruction during the small-group sessions, the collaboration and dialogue within the book clubs, and learner presentations in the whole-class setting all contribute to the learner's independent learning.

Independent learners apply all the strategies they have learned to continue to form questions, consider multiple viewpoints, and evaluate what they have read. This process now happens not only with others but also within themselves. Through discussion and dialogue, learners learn to conduct a "dialogue in their minds" to continue to think about ideas even when they read alone (Calkins, p. 75). This independent individual learning is a goal for all of the interaction paths.

Our society needs thoughtful citizens who can question, evaluate, and interpret the deluge of information that is part of the fabric of our society. Working collaboratively to empower learners to seek innovative solutions to the challenges we face as a society is the responsibility of all citizens. Part of the answer to the challenges society faces lies in the commitment of educators to teach our learners the importance of applying the principles of evaluative literacy to today's world. One critical component of assisting learners acquire and practice evaluative literacy lies in the structure of lessons.

Lesson Structure and Content

Earlier in this chapter, the Gradual Release of Responsibility Model (Pearson & Gallagher, 1983) was discussed as a framework for sharing responsibility with learners. This model can provide guidance to embed the principles of effective instruction into lessons designed to teach evaluative literacy. Below is a discussion of how each of the four stages in the Gradual Release of Responsibility Model can be aligned with the various sections in a lesson.

1. Teacher modeling and explanation of strategy

    At the beginning of the lesson, the educator takes time to explain the strategy by making her thinking public. During this introduction, the educator explicitly states the strategy and explains the reasons why this specific strategy is effective. In many ways, this part of the lesson is anticipatory in nature by setting the stage for what is to come.

2. Guided practice

    This second part of the lesson is where the educator "scaffolds" the learning. This scaffolding reflects what Vygotsky has termed the Zone of Proximal Development. This zone or stage of learning represents that

time when a learner is learning to do something with help from an educator to be able to do it without any help. Vygotsky stated that "what a child
can do with assistance today, she will be able to do by herself tomorrow"
(1978, p. 87).

During this time, learners are invited to practice a strategy during
whole-class discussions, are asked to apply it in pairs or small groups,
and are encouraged to learn from the feedback of both the educator and
skilled peers. This feedback is offered in a collaborative, caring manner
that respects each learner and highlights the positive aspects as well as
identifying specific ways the learner progress. This is the time in the lesson when learners experience scaffolded instruction.

3. Independent practice accompanied by feedback

By this stage, learners have demonstrated flexibility in their thinking,
and they can now apply the strategy more independently. This is the time
in the lesson to allow learners a greater degree of responsibility and allow
them to practice the strategy more independently. Educator feedback is
critical during this stage to let the learners know when they are applying the
strategy effectively, correct mistakes when they occur, and challenge the
learners to articulate the ways the strategy is helping their understanding.

4. Application

This stage is often described as the "Aha" moment when the lightbulb
metaphorically goes on, and the learner can apply the strategy independently. Learners can now articulate the way the strategy is helping them
construct meaning and deepen their understanding. This is the time in
the lesson when learners are provided with the opportunity to apply the
strategy to other materials effectively.

LESSON SUBSTANCE

In addition to the process for instruction following the Gradual Release
Model, giving purpose, clarity, and guidance, the educator must also consider
the material used for its substance, difficulty level, complexity, and format. It
is also wise to address socio-cultural concerns to accommodate varied background experiences.

CHOOSING THE TEXT

Readers benefit from engaging with a wide range of books. One factor to
consider when choosing texts is the level of difficulty, which is dependent on
various factors such as the reader's background, ability, motivation, as well
as the text's complexity and format. When choosing material, the educator

should ask several questions related to the lesson's purpose. One such question is, *Am I choosing this text to model and explain a specific strategy?* If so, the text will be read aloud and can be a challenging text since the learner will be listening rather than reading independently.

Part of teaching evaluative literacy strategies is teaching learners to listen carefully, understand deeply, and respond thoughtfully. When educators are modeling and explaining strategies, the focus will be on listening and sharing ideas. This modeling by the educator provides the whole class with the opportunity to observe the tools of evaluative literacy and join in with the educator to try the strategies.

A second question is, *"Am I choosing this text to scaffold instruction and allow the learner opportunity to practice the strategy?"* If so, the text should be at an instructional level so that the learners can read fairly independently yet simultaneously benefit from support and guidance from an educator or peers. A third question is, *"Am I choosing this text to allow the learner an opportunity to practice the strategy independently?"* If so, the text should be at an independent level so that the learners can work independently to gain understanding as to the ways using evaluative literacy strategies effectively helps deepen our understanding.

While educators' understanding of how different levels of text difficulty can effectively be utilized to teach evaluative literacy strategies, an educator's understanding of the power of stories and the complexity of text structures is also important. Texts need to be sufficiently complex to prompt nuanced thinking. Complex sentences and paragraph structure challenge the reader to delve deeper to read evaluatively.

Controversial text can also help develop critical, evaluative thinking because it forces the reader to consider their own thinking. For readers of diverse backgrounds, the text also needs to be balanced between familiar and unfamiliar socio-cultural backgrounds for sufficient understanding.

In sum, both the application of well-planned organization of a teaching process embedded in clear, purposeful instruction and a text that exposes learners to the beauty and power of words constitute good lesson structure and content to encourage evaluation in literacy work.

These ideas apply to traditional text and media as ways to develop skills in evaluative literacy. What may be helpful here are several examples for instruction in both environments, traditional text, and media, based upon the twenty characteristics presented in Chapter 1.

SAMPLE LESSONS

The sample lessons fall into three categories for some of the twenty characteristics of evaluative literacy identified in Chapter 1 and the ideas on media from Chapter 2. The lessons are numbered to correspond to those character-istics. Some of the characteristics, although listed separately here, may be adapted to traditional or digital texts. The categories are as follows:

1. Category 1: Traditional Text
2. Category 2: Digital Texts
3. Category 3: Combined and Independent Texts

The samples in each category integrate the instructional principles presented earlier in this chapter with the characteristics of each lesson.

To give you a sense of what instruction would be like, we have developed three categories of lessons. Category 1 illustrates lessons for traditional text. Category 2 illustrates lessons for digital text and electronic/digital media. Category 3 represents a synthesis of traditional and digital/media work. We have tried to illustrate instruction here with examples for many of the twenty characteristics so that you can see how our ideas work in practice.

SAMPLE LESSONS

CATEGORY 1: TRADITIONAL TEXT

#2 Reading for Intention and Assumptions

Using Magazine and Newspaper Advertisements

Step 1: Collect a number of different magazine and newspaper advertisements selling a particular type of product (different brands).

Step 2: Have the learners identify the explicit message promoted by each ad

Step 3: The learners and the educator should discuss the meaning of words such as "suggestion," "imply," "connotation," and "association."

Step 4: The learners should articulate the implicit "message behind the message" contained in certain ads and identify the components of the ad which suggest the message. The learners should identify the connection between the product and the association implied in the ad and describe as precisely as possible the elements of the ad which make the connection.

Step 5: Have the learners compare how different makers of the same type of product use different images to convey the same implicit theme or message.

Step 6: Have learners make collages of advertisements organized around a particular theme (sex appeal, romance, success, sophistication, fun, family togetherness, health, masculinity/feminity, etc.) Share with the class in a bulletin board display.

#5 Teaching How to Read for a Point of View

Using Poems on the Same Topic

Step 1: In this activity, the educator will find several poems on the same topic where the author has different feelings about the topic (i.e., a particular animal, season, hobby, and holiday).

Step 2: Before reading the poems, have each learner jot down a few words or phrases that best capture the way they feel about the topic.

Step 3: Learners will read the poems chosen by the educator silently, and then volunteers will read them aloud.

Step 4: As a class, generate a list of keywords or phrases that best describes the author's point of view on the topic.

Step 5: Ask learners to share the lists they generated in Step 2. Discuss how different points of view on a topic can change the mood or the message obtained from the poem.

Step 6: Choose a poem where descriptive words play an important role in demonstrating the author's point of view. Type the poem leaving blanks for key description words allowing the learners to fill in the blanks with words that make sense.

Step 7: Ask learners to share the poems that they created. Discuss how descriptive words are essential in conveying the author's point of view in poetry.

#8 Constructing an Opposing Point of View

A: Evaluating a Hypothetical Proposal

Step 1: Develop a hypothetical proposal that the entire class will discuss. (i.e., There will not be any athletic department in this school any longer).

Step 2: Give the learners guidelines and together brainstorm why the proposal is not a good idea.

Step 3: As a class, learners should give reasons, short-term and long-term effects of such a decision and support their thoughts and feelings about the proposal.

Step 4: Have the learners find articles about other schools that may have faced a similar decision. Learners should read and consider them.

Step 5: Write a formal proposal, as a class, presenting their opposing point of view.

B: Analyzing a Short Story with Multiple Interpretations

Step 1: Give the learners a short story that may lead to multiple interpretations of the text.

Step 2: Ask the learners to read the story for a potential interpretation of a character's major decision in the text.

Step 3: Have the learners write contradictory explanations for the character's behavior and decision. Each point of view should be justified with examples from the text.

Step 4: Through discussion, have the learner show how each point of view does or does not support a particular interpretation of the theme of the story.

#7 Sorting Personal Feelings from Application of External Criteria

A: Developing Criteria for Evaluating a Short Story

Step 1: Have learners read a short story by an author such as Thurber, Poe, etc.

Step 2: Have learners brainstorm criteria for evaluating the story.

Step 3: Discuss the ideas and determine the specific criteria to be used in evaluating the story that separates personal feelings from the criteria as identified.

Step 4: Have learners form groups and evaluate the story according to the criteria.

Step 5: Have each learner write a story and evaluate it using the same criteria.

Step 6: Have learners form the same groups and evaluate one of the learners' stories.

Step 7: Discuss the process of evaluation with the entire class. Ask which piece of writing was easier to evaluate objectively and why.

B: Bringing Prior Knowledge of Disabled Individuals to the Evaluation

Step 1: Assess prior knowledge of disabled individuals by having each learner answer a survey of their knowledge and experience with disabled individuals. Discuss their feelings about disabled individuals.

Step 2: Have learners read the story "Architectural Barriers Take on a New Meaning" by Larz Neilson.

Step 3: Have each learner evaluate the story using these criteria: (1) language elements such as diction, connotation, and denotation, (2) style of writing and its effects on the message, (3) structural elements, and (4) thematic elements.

Step 4: Match the evaluations of the text with learners' prior knowledge and feelings about disabled individuals.

Step 5: Determine through discussion if there was any correlation between the learners who liked the story and their prior knowledge and feelings about disabled individuals.

Step 6: Discuss the process of evaluating text critically when personal feelings are involved. How do the readers keep personal feelings from interfering with an objective reading of a text?

#9 Drawing Conclusions, Making Predictions, and Suspending Judgment through Maintaining Tentativeness and Hypothesis Testing

Using Characters in a Play to Make Predictions and Draw Conclusions

Step 1: Read aloud in class a play with three to four major characters, but stop before reading the last act.

Step 2: Have learners form groups and determine how the play should end. If consensus in a group cannot be reached, groups may be rearranged so that all learners in each group can come to a reasonable agreement on their version of the ending.

Step 3: Have each group present their version of the last act. They should write it out in summary form and then script it. Let the learners act out the script.

Step 4: Reach a class consensus on the best last act. Groups must explain how they withheld judgment or changed their mind about each version.

Step 5: Discuss the process of reaching a consensus about each last act.

#13 Establishing Reader's Goals

Using Informative and Expository Text Form to Evaluate an Article

Step 1: Select an article that is informative in nature and expository in style and form.

Step 2: Have the learners survey the article with the goal of generating prereading questions about the content and the form of the text.

Step 3: Before reading, have the learners share their prereading questions with the class. Select five questions that will establish the readers' goals for reading.

Step 4: Have the learners read the passage with these questions in mind. Discuss answers to the questions.

Step 5: Have the learners reread the text without the specific questions to see if there are other or more important points made.

Step 6: Discuss what the learners have gleaned from the second reading and compare it to the first reading.

CATEGORY 2: DIGITAL TEXT

#14 Detecting Deception

Step 1: Explain the differences between fact, opinion, misinformation, and disinformation.

Step 2: Introduce learners to fact-checking sites and have them practice using them with examples you provide. (Make sure to include reputable sources, as well as examples of misinformation and disinformation.)
- FactCheck.org
- Politifact.com
- Snopes.com
- Media Bias Fact Check
- Allsides Media Bias Chart https://www.allsides.com/media-bias/media-bias-chart
- Ad fontes Media Bias Chart(https://adfontesmedia.com

Step 3: Discuss their findings as a class. Which media is credible? Which is not? Which were most difficult to identify? Were there any cases of deception they missed?

#15 Seeking Credibility and Validity

Step 1: Share and discuss The Center for Media Literacy's Five Core Concepts:
- All media messages are constructed.
- Media messages are constructed using creative language with its own rules.
- Different people experience the same media message differently.
- Media have embedded values and points of view.
- Most media messages are organized to gain profit and/or power.

Step 2: Explain the terms bias, implicit bias, and explicit bias, and give examples of how these are found in media today.

Step 3: Teach learners the process of lateral reading. Give them a sample online news article from a reputable source and another from a source of disinformation. Walk them through opening multiple web browser tabs as they research their source. They should examine the author and the publisher of each news article and then check for any bias.
- Is the information being communicated by an established news outlet?
- Or is it an independent source, such as a blogger or citizen journalist?
- Always check to see if there is an "about us" page if it is a website or a link to a bio if it is on social media.
- Use fact-checking and bias evaluation tools for each piece:
- FactCheck.org
- Politifact.com
- Snopes.com
- Media Bias Fact Check
- Allsides Media Bias Chart https://www.allsides.com/media-bias/media-bias-chart
- Ad Fontes Media Bias Charthttps://adfontesmedia.com

Step 4: Choose a topic that is current and has opposing viewpoints. Then, choose several kinds of media in different formats (TV news story, print advertisement, a social media post such as a TikTok video or tweet, and audio podcast) that cover this topic. Make sure they represent different viewpoints, and ideally, find some that share misinformation.

Step 5: Have learners evaluate each media you selected. (This can be done in groups or individually.) Learners should critically analyze each media message, examining media length, images, sounds, links to more information, references to sources, interviews, etc. Have them note similarities and differences between the types of coverage in each media genre. (This is a good time to have them practice their lateral reading skills.)

- Have learners consider the author/producer of each media. What is their background? Are they part of a news organization or professional media outlet? How are they financed?
- Have learners identify the purpose of the communication—is it to persuade? To take action? To inform?
- Have learners consider the target audience—who is this media made for or directed to? How would folks outside this audience feel when viewing this media?
- Have learners examine the content for bias—Is there a particular message that the media is expressing that supports one opinion over the other? Or does it remain factual and impartial?
- Have them explore medium-specific questions. For example, if looking at a video, have them analyze the visuals and audio; if it is a print ad, have them critique the images and text.
- Have them verify the content of the media: Is it fact? Opinion? Misinformation? Disinformation? Make sure they use fact-checking sites:

Step 6: Discuss their findings as a class. Which media is credible? Which is not? Evaluate the unique strengths and drawbacks of each type of media source. Questions to consider:

- How does the coverage of your topic in your sources compare? What is similar? What patterns or themes emerge between all types of media?
- In what ways does the coverage in your sources differ? What ideas are left out? What specific information emerges in one source that is not lifted up in another source? What information is left out or remains unaddressed from the sources altogether? What rationale would you give for why certain information is not included?
- Consider the type of media each source falls into. What are the strengths and drawbacks of each media format? (For example, if one of your sources is a magazine article from The Atlantic and an interview posted on YouTube by the Jubilee network, what are the strengths and drawbacks of each format: online magazine vs. YouTube video interview)

#16 Developing Sensitivity to Language

Step 1: Introduce learners to the concept of "loaded language." (For example, "gay marriage" instead of "marriage equality," "illegal alien" instead of "undocumented immigrant.") Explain and demonstrate how loaded language is a form of bias, as well as predisposes people to particular viewpoints.

Step 2: Have learners practice identifying loaded language using examples you have collected from a variety of media sources.

Step 3: Have learners create a slideshow or posterboard using examples of the loaded language they found in the media. They should include a statement about why each term is "loaded."

CATEGORY 3: COMBINED AND INDEPENDENT TEXT

#7 Sorting Personal Feelings from Application of External Criteria

Step 1: Have learners watch a video that shows just one point of view in a story. (A great one to use is the story of the three little pigs. https://www.youtube.com/watch?v=FNYBQsay_Ek)

Step 2: Have the learners discuss their feelings about the characters and the story. Who was right? Who was wrong? Why?

Step 3: Now show learners the opposing viewpoint. (https://www.youtube.com/watch?v=vB07RfntTvw&t=416s)

Step 4: Ask the learners if their perspective has changed. Who was right? Who was wrong? Why?

Step 5: Remind learners that although they will be tempted to let personal feelings and initial judgments cloud their evaluation of a source, they should take their time to seek out multiple perspectives when presented with new information. (High school learners can watch this video for a better look at what comprehensive evidence gathering looks like: https://youtu.be/vDGrfhJH1P4.)

#17 Building Knowledge Bases and
#18 Developing Schema for Reflective Questioning

Step 1: Explain the traditional methods of knowledge building (books, magazines, journal articles, etc.) and newer methods (Internet search, online databases, ebooks, etc.). Cover the pros and cons of each source, as well as best practices for finding information about a particular topic.

Step 2: This assignment can be done individually or in groups. Have learners choose a topic or assign a topic, whichever works best for your class and curriculum. Explain that they will search for a variety of sources, including traditional print media, electronic media, and digital media.

Step 3: Allow the learners time to search for their sources. As they do so, they should apply their skills in detecting deception and seeking credibility and validity. They should choose three to four sources they have determined to be credible and use these sources to build their knowledge base.

Step 4: Learners should create a multimedia presentation explaining their topic. This could be a PowerPoint presentation, a podcast, a short video, or a blog. They should provide an overview of the topic and then compare and contrast the strengths of their chosen media sources.

Step 5: Have learners complete a written reflection about their process. What did they learn? Was credible information difficult to find? Why or why not? How did they decide which sources to trust and incorporate into their presentation? Did any of the information they learned challenge their previous understanding of the topic? What would they do differently next time?

#19 Achieving Automaticity of Analysis and
#20 Generating Responses to Text: Outcomes of Literacy

This assessment should be completed *after* learners have had ample time to develop their literacy skills, particularly with new media.

Step 1: Provide learners with three to five different media sources that cover the same news story. (For example, a podcast, a newspaper article, and a Tweet.) Choose sources of varying degrees of credibility.

Step 2: Learners should evaluate and verify the credibility, reliability, and transparency, as well as identify the content and context of each source. (To judge automaticity, learners should not have access to checklists or worksheets – they should be able to remember the steps of analysis without assistance.)

Step 3: Learners should compare and contrast the three sources. Which sources would they recommend to someone who wanted to know more about the new story? Why? Which would they not share? Why? This activity will push them to integrate schemas and cognitive activities that come with the responsible communication of individual and collective thought.

These examples illustrate our discussion in Chapters 1 and 2 on evaluative literacy and the digital world. Our goal in the next chapter on assessment is to take some of these examples and apply them as assessments. These instructional lessons are also appropriate for assessment tasks, particularly projects, and portfolios. As we move into the next chapter, we see how instruction is integrated into the assessment.

CHAPTER SUMMARY

Given appropriate instruction, learners will develop the evaluative skills necessary for literacy in our changing world. Although the media landscape is fast-changing, the underlying skills needed to evaluate media are more concrete. Working first through traditional print media and then new (digital) media will allow learners the time to build and hone their evaluative literacy.

Chapter 4

The Many Faces of Assessment

OVERVIEW

In this chapter, we consider how literacy initiatives and the factors that influence them reveal some serious implications and the need for changes in assessing literacy proficiency. We do so by examining previous and present assessment practices and specific ways the digital world requires changes in these practices. We identify themes in the research and the initiatives on assessment issues and measures that reflect ongoing work and can guide future work. In doing so, we hope that we can suggest a viable direction and solutions for broadening our view of assessment.

GUIDING QUESTIONS

Are there historical perspectives related to assessment that can offer insight into the need for developing relevant assessment measures to match current and emerging forms of literacy?

Can we classify and describe each type of assessment and its limitations and advantages?

How does a changing concept of literacy influence a broadening view of assessment?

What are the driving forces for changes in assessment measures?

Are there principles for assessment to guide future work?

Can we develop a model for various levels of education and diverse cognitive and sociological groups for assessing literacy proficiency that integrates changes in instruction and the principles of assessment that have occurred over the years of the literacy periods and the media literacy evolution eras?

SHIFTING TO ASSESSMENT

The companion to instruction is assessment as a means for determining how effective instruction has been in achieving proficiency in literacy at different stages of development and in a digital world in general. Tracing past and present forms of assessment and their limitations in a digital world should help us to see any relationship between instruction and assessment as we move into the future. We then move on to explore emerging initiatives in research and assessment to resolve these concerns and to give us a vision for the future for coupling instruction and assessment.

In this chapter, the words teacher and student are used to refer to historical applications of assessment, whereas the words educator and learner are used to reflect our broadened view of literacy.

HISTORICAL PERSPECTIVE ON ASSESSMENT

A look at early and some present measures will show their limitations for assessing newer expectations for evaluating literacy proficiency in an ever-changing world. In doing so, we look at how these assessment forms are changing along with the impetus for the changes. Our concern with earlier assessments raises several questions to be addressed here. Questions such as When and Why did assessment start? What was it like? Who created it? Why was it used? should guide our understanding of societal expectations for literacy proficiency.

Reading Assessment: 1900–1940s

Interest in understanding the reading process and concerns over students' reading ability led to the development in the early 1900s of the first published reading assessments. These early assessments served three general purposes. The tests screened students for general reading ability; they identified areas of weakness in reading performance and provided information about the nature of the reading process. These efforts were helpful precursors to initial research efforts to measure and improve success in reading instruction.

Specific Assessments

The first standardized reading assessment was published in 1915 by William S. Gray. The Gray Reading Test assessed a student's oral reading ability and determined areas of reading weaknesses. The test results were used to design reading instruction in the areas of weakness for struggling readers (Gray, 1917).

While the Gray test was administered individually and identified areas of reading weakness, there was a need for group-administered reading assessment. The Kansas Silent Reading Test was published in 1916 by Kelly. As a whole class screening test, the Kansas Silent Reading Test was the first published comprehension test and the first to use a multiple-choice format (Pearson & Hamm, 2005; Sammacca et al., 2016). The test shifted attention to silent reading from oral reading.

The reading screener was quick to administer in a whole class setting and easy to score. Both tests (Gray and Kelly) were used to identify areas of weakness in reading performance and to design instruction for struggling readers. The concern for struggling readers was the focus of the work in reading and was called remedial reading. The beliefs and assumptions were that everyone could attain minimal proficiency in reading and that a minimal level of proficiency was adequate.

Interest in the reading process led Thorndike (1917) to publish a book that used informal reading assessment to explain what was occurring inside a reader's brain during the reading process (Pearson & Hamm, 2005). This use of reading assessment in the early part of the twentieth century saw the beginning of what Pearson described as the reading research world's "quest to get as close as possible to the phenomenological act of comprehension as it occurs" (Pearson & Hamm, 2005, p. 16). This broadened the purpose of assessment measures and generated an ongoing concern for research on reading processes that returned to Huey's original interest and work of 1908 in the psychology of reading (Huey, 1908).

Even with a heightened interest in reading processes, reading assessment in the 1920s saw a continued focus on reading comprehension tests as screeners and sorters of students with reading difficulties. Concurrently, diagnostic reading assessments continued to be developed to shed light on the areas of weakness for readers, with Gates adding a diagnostic assessment in 1927 (Pearson & Hamm, 2005; Sammacca et al., 2016).

Individually administered Informal Reading Inventories were developed in the 1930s and 1940s. These reading assessments were analyzed for how students processed text, often called miscue analysis. Further use of the miscue analysis procedure resurfaced in the 1960s under the influence of psycholinguistics, only to be overshadowed by the earlier types of assessment on struggling readers and the reading process. Reading fluency was also the focus of the work by Gates in 1937, and error patterns were the focus of the tests created by Durrell and Betts in 1937 and 1946, respectively (Pearson & Hamm, 2005).

There was a slight shift in assessment in the early 1950s. Having been a pioneer in assessment for the first half of the twentieth century, Gray embarked on a four-year project for the United Nations that attempted to describe the worldwide state of literacy. The United Nations, like Gray, felt that universal literacy was the direction that the world's countries should work toward (Simon, 1956; Gray, 1969), given the competitiveness of the international environment in many arenas.

Our path describing literacy assessment in the digital age journeys in that direction also. Here, we turn to explore the evolution of literacy assessment in international and national initiatives after we describe the substance of early and present measures of the tests used.

ASSESSMENTS DURING THE FIVE LITERACY PERIODS AND FIVE MEDIA ERAS

Looking at assessment measures that reflect the levels of literacy proficiency and the changes that have occurred over the five periods of literacy (1947 to present) and the five eras of media literacy (pre-1500 BCE to present) presented in Chapters 1 and 2 will help us see the developing need for a transformation of future assessment measures.

Substance of Early and Present Measures

Assessments used during the first three periods of literacy focused on brief print text with a focus on basic literacy. They were administered at several levels of achievement, often twice a year, to get pre/post-improvement measures over time. They tended to be a series of brief passages and several questions that usually were text-based, with a minor bit of inferential reading required.

There were some changes in substance as the texts were administered at different proficiency levels. However, the tests seldom assessed higher-order thinking ability, as described in Chapter 1. Nor did they include any assessment of the media literacy that began to emerge during the fourth and fifth periods of the literacy periods.

Often, these standardized tests have been used for the comparative performance of groups of readers of proficiency within the country. Sometimes, these assessments have been used to make cross-cultural comparisons even when the equivalency of the instruments has not been established. Often too, the tests were not aligned with grade-level instruction where the test formats needed to reflect classroom practices. This often induces a prior-to-test-taking mentality of teaching for the test rather than addressing and assessing the types of learning that more often occur in classrooms. Sometimes, too, it limits what teachers do in the classroom to have students simply be ready to take the tests.

Recently, assessment tools have looked to make cross-country comparisons with assessment instruments. These cross-country comparisons reflect the competition in the environment where we live. However, they still fall short of assessing higher-order thinking abilities, such as the kind of evaluation we are encouraging. They seldom address the requirements of our changing times and society.

Many tests follow this basic structure to allow for standardization to be developed for comparison across individuals and groups of individuals. However, the tests tend not to have sufficient diagnostic measures for improving individual proficiency even when there is an item analysis of the test items. Again, the answers to comprehension items tend to be closely text-based. There has been some effort to broaden the subject content of test passages, but they are still not diverse enough for the varied populations of examinees in our schools and society in general.

Where there has been an interest in individual performance, informal inventories and more diagnostic tests have been developed. They attempt to determine the individual's comprehension of messages through listening ability and then compare it to reading ability. There also has been some attempt to determine the ability of specific skills.

All of this testing has been based upon a skills-based model of comprehension and the assumption that if individuals have these individual skills, they can read the materials and texts they encounter in real-life situations. This is a questionable assumption and may not be adequate for literacy in the emerging digital world.

Transforming Measures: Emerging Efforts

As we moved into the fourth and fifth literacy periods and later media eras, literacy initiatives have attempted to develop global and international standardization and, even more recently, to develop measures considering literacy in digital environments. Our goal is to delineate and characterize the substance and themes found in various levels of literacy proficiency to illustrate variations and changes that are occurring and the expectations that they are creating. Where possible, we hope to identify what factors influence these expectations and changes and their implications.

WHERE ARE WE HEADED NOW?

The more recent literacy initiatives and efforts have occurred on several levels, creating increased expectations and assessments for performance as we have moved into the digital world. These initiatives appear to be at several levels. The first is at a global level, and the second is at multiple national levels.

At the global level, we see a broad initiative influenced by economic conditions and organizations interested in economic development. At the national level, we see individual work in separate regions and countries and, more specifically, in the United States. Within the US initiatives, we see national standardization across the states, within individual states, and at district and classroom levels.

We do see that in the work that is emerging based upon a broadening view of literacy that there are attempts to transform some of these earlier assessment tools to include skills with digital technologies. These changes that are occurring at several levels—global, national, state, districtwide, and classroom levels may best be understood by examining the research and specific measures that suggest themes that permeate the changes and suggest future measures for evaluating literacy proficiency. They will be addressed here in preparation for a model to direct future assessment measures to understand the implications for comparison at all levels and to shape future work.

ASSESSMENT IN THE DIGITAL AGE

Literacy Assessment in the Digital Age begins to serve several purposes: (1) it shows where students are performing in relation to learning/curriculum standards; (2) it helps determine where students are developmentally on the continuum of becoming literacy proficient in the digital environment; (3) it informs instruction; (4) it provides feedback on instructional programs and curriculum implementation.

Within these four purposes of assessment, five themes are emerging that help frame the assessment world in the digital environment. This section will describe the five themes and explain some recent literacy initiatives and research to demonstrate how they are incorporated into the emerging concept of literacy.

The five themes are:

(1) Literacy Assessment Flows from The Comprehension Process
(2) Literacy Assessment is a Student-Centered, Teacher-Involved Process
(3) Literacy Assessment Involves Expanding Measurement Components and Focus
(4) Literacy Assessment is Evolutionary in Nature
(5) Technology in Literacy Assessment Can Help Counter Low SES and Disabilities

---

Figure 4.1   Themes for Assessing an Emerging Concept of Literacy.

THEME 1: LITERACY ASSESSMENT FLOWS
FROM THE COMPREHENSION PROCESS

The first theme is that literacy assessment flows from the processes used to construct meaning when reading in our current multi-modal, online/digital environment (Ruday & Caprino, 2023; Henry, 2012; Chen et al., 2012; Leu et al., 2008).

Constructing meaning in the online/digital environment is accomplished through a series of processes that help a reader make sense of the multiple sources of information encountered in the online/digital world. This processing of text involves ways that are at times similar to processing traditional text and, at other times, employs traditional text/learning processes in the service of constructing meaning in the uniqueness of the online/digital environment. These processes work together to enable the reader to build a deep understanding of the material encountered in the digital world.

Text processing in the online/digital world begins with the foundational reading processing skills of word recognition, vocabulary knowledge, comprehension strategies, and responding to what has been read while constructing meaning (Leu, Kinzer et al., 2013). The processes involved in constructing meaning in the online/digital environment then expand to additional processes that reflect processing text through the cognitive perspective, evaluative literacy perspective, engagement and motivation perspectives, and the sociocultural perspective.

We have identified nine processes readers engage in when constructing meaning in the online/digital world. They group together in the literacy perspectives in the following way.

The processes that readers engage in when constructing meaning in the online world are summarized in figure 4.2.

Each of these nine processes helps readers construct meaning and understand what is encountered in the online/digital world. Here, we will explore them further.

COGNITIVE PERSPECTIVE

Finding and locating information processes: At the beginning level of engagement with the online/digital environment, a reader searches for and locates information. This information can come in multi-modal forms: extended text, short/caption text, visual (pictures and images), and auditory. A reader processes these sources of information while constructing an understanding of what is being read. The processes of locating information involve navigating the search procedure, reading web pages, following links, and accessing information from various online multi-mode sources (Leu, Kinzer et al., 2013).

Processes for Constructing Meaning

Cognitive Perspective

1. Finding and locating information processes
2. Creating a summary/synthesis processes

Evaluative Literacy Perspective

3. Evaluating the information read processes

Engagement and Motivation Perspective

4. Engagement processes (personal engagement with constructing and understanding meaning of the digital world they are exploring)
5. Collaboration processes—enhancing comprehension through collaboration and co-operation
6. Creating processes—creating an understanding and representation of the material encountered online
7. Communication processes—communicating your response to online/digital explorations

Sociocultural Perspective

8. Belonging/connection processes
9. Scaffolding learning processes (Vygotsky's knowledgeable guide/zone of proximal development)

Figure 4.2   Processes for Constructing Meaning.

Summarizing/synthesizing information processes: After locating and reading information online from multiple sources and multiple modalities, a reader enters into the process of summarizing and synthesizing the information (Leu, Kinzer et al., 2013). In the summarizing and synthesis process, a reader constructs their own text of what has been read in a process of integrating key ideas into broader concepts of a message.

Evaluative Literacy Perspective

Evaluating information processes: To create a summary/synthesis of the information found online, a reader has to evaluate the information that has been located (Leu, Kinzer et al., 2013). The evaluation process involves determining what sources of information should be included and what is worth listening to. The process also involves evaluating the reasoning and underlying assumptions in the text. The type of critical evaluation employed may be a source of some of the differences between traditional text and online processing of print (Leu, Kinzer, et al., 2013).

ENGAGEMENT AND MOTIVATION PERSPECTIVE

Engagement and motivation processes: Navigating through the multitude of sources of information that a reader encounters in the online/digital world calls for the reader to be self-directed and motivated to engage in the reading process. In this environment, self-direction and engagement processes come to the foreground. There is a personal drive to find things out. Constructing and understanding what is found and constructing a meaningful understanding of the world become central parts of the processing that occurs in reading in this world. As part of this engagement, curiosity becomes an important factor in successful engagement and reading in the digital world (Peng et al., 2021).

Collaborating processes: Reading online and in the digital environment offers collaboration opportunities. Collaboration usually provides emotional support for readers. Processing text collaboratively has also been found to enhance comprehension by bringing multiple perspectives to work (Leu, Kinzer et al., 2013). Collaboration is not only parceling parts of a larger text to an individual. It requires constant exchange of reading, writing, conceptualizing, and critiquing of ideas of all collaborators.

Creating processes: Engaging with the online/digital world involves a series of creating processes. First, a reader creates a plan to investigate a topic. After reading and collecting information on the topic, the reader creates a synthesis/summary of the information. Creating processes can stop at that point in the reading process, but often, the creating process goes on to the next step, where the reader develops a product representing their understanding, reactions, and evaluation of the material in the online/digital world.

Communication: The creating processes can lead to deciding whether or not to share the information the reader has created in the digital space. The communication processes involve deciding how to share what has been created for the reading experience (what platform, social media, etc.), with whom to share it, and the openness of feedback. By sharing their reaction and understandings of the texts read, the communication processes help the reader make the material their own as well as open up the possibility for the reader to expand their thinking on the topic through the feedback that comes.

SOCIOCULTURAL PERSPECTIVE

Belonging to a community/connection process: Closely related to the communication processes is an aspect of processing text digitally that we call belonging to the community/connection processes. Reading in the online/digital world involves the process of coming into contact with others and finding a place of belonging in the digital environment. This experience of connection and belonging through engagement with the online/digital world enhances a reader's understanding of the material that has been read and helps the reader build confidence in their interpretation of the material.

Finding a community for belonging in the online/digital world has helped to pave the way for further, deeper engagement with difficult topics in the digital world (Lammers & Astuti, 2020; Brownell & Sheridan, 2020). This enhances the reader's attempts to construct an effective understanding of their world through digital exploration.

Scaffolding processes: Support for readers constructing meaning in the online/digital world includes providing instructional scaffolding that involves sociocultural processes. Digital texts are being constructed in ways that support readers in ways that are similar to what an adult (or more knowledgeable reader) does to support a younger reader reading a text. The digital supports can mirror the scaffolding that the adult could provide to help facilitate a younger reader constructing meaning from the digital text. These supports include asking the child questions about what will happen next in the story and providing background information to make the text more accessible.

This type of digital support creates a Vygotskian-like framework of an experienced guide leading an apprentice reader. In this case, the experienced guide is digital. The reader's comprehension of the text is enhanced by engaging in the sociocultural processes provided through digital scaffolding (Furenes et al., 2021). Specific international and national initiatives support these nine processes.

SPECIFIC INITIATIVES

Literacy initiatives representing international and national organizations have supported using processing skills as a foundation of digital literacy assessment. The countries representing the largest economies in the world, called the G20 countries, have called for creating a digital assessment that reflects a broad definition of digital literacy (Chetty et al., 2017). Guided by the UN's definition of digital literacy (Law et al., 2018; Karpati, 2011), the G20 promotes creating digital literacy assessments that reflect the processes involved in constructing meaning in digital environments.

Other international organizations such as UNESCO, the International Telecommunications Union, and World Education Inc. also have encouraged a focus on digital processing skills when assessing digital literacy skills (Law et al., 2018; Karpati, 2011; Coward et al., 2020; World Education Inc, 2022; ISTE, 2022).

Current large-scale international literacy assessments such as PIRLS and PISA include simulated online environment reading tasks (OECD, 2021; TIMSS &PIRLS International Study Center, 2022). These tasks are focused on the processing skills involved in constructing meaning in an online environment. On the national level, the NAEP assessment moved to a digitally based assessment format in 2017. The 2026 Assessment Framework describes literacy tasks that will include simulated online reading tasks that focus on reading processing skills involved in constructing meaning in an online environment with a particular emphasis on evaluating and synthesizing (US DOE, 2021).

On the national level, multiple literacy initiatives also have been promoted, including processing skills as part of digital literacy assessments. Digital Resilience in American Workforce, Rework America Business Network (2019), National Educators Association (Murray, 2020), along with the US Department of Education (LINCS, 2022), and several state and statewide initiatives, such as California (2008) and Massachusetts (ACLS, 2022), are doing this work. In general, following comprehension processes seems key to understanding literacy proficiency, and assessment seems important.

THEME 2: LITERACY ASSESSMENT IS A STUDENT-CENTERED, TEACHER-INVOLVED PROCESS

The second theme is that literacy assessment is a student-centered, interactive process between the administrator of the assessment and the students being assessed. It includes project-based assessment and a high level of teacher involvement in the decision-making process (Forzani et al., 2020; Castek & Coiro, 2015).

A primary purpose of assessment in the online/digital environment is to determine the stage of literacy development for student performance as well as to determine the degree of proficiency that students have in the processing involved in constructing meaning in the digital world. Engaging students in project-based assessment tasks creates a student-friendly assessment environment that helps accomplish this task by determining acquisition and processing strategies in a natural, student-centered environment. It also is more likely to mirror instructional practices that integrate skills as a goal.

The role of the teacher here revolves around a higher degree of interaction with the assessments and with the students than in the traditional assessment world. In the online/digital assessment environment, teachers are involved in designing, developing, and selecting project-based learning tasks that can be integrated into their curriculum and then assessed accordingly.

Teachers are also involved in interpreting the results of the assessment project-based tasks and determining the nature of the instruction that should precede or follow the assessment. Here, according to Eyal (2012), the teacher moves away from the role of simply administering the assessment to taking a central role in assessing portfolio assessment, online peer assessment, and text-making in the digital environment; thus, taking a more active role.

Forzani, Corrigan, and Slump (2020) describe creating student-centered assessments in the digital environment that enable students to become co-collaborators with teachers in the assessment process and critical consumers of the online/digital content they engage. Further, current literacy initiatives demonstrate that literacy assessment in the digital world can be student-centered and inclusive of a dynamic role for the teacher. The University of Connecticut's ORCA project describes using student-centered performance-based tasks and portfolios in digital literacy assessment (Leu, Kulikowich et al., 2013; Leu et al., 2008).

In general, developing assessment measures will mirror present and hopefully better instructional practices more closely than in earlier versions of assessment work.

THEME 3: LITERACY ASSESSMENT INVOLVES EXPANDING MEASUREMENT COMPONENTS AND FOCUS

The third theme is that literacy assessment involves expanding measurement components and focus. It involves both quantitative and qualitative measures to give comparative and diagnostic information. This is an enhancement of traditional measures that generally are group comparisons with some item analysis that may help to show individual performance. Adding a qualitative dimension captures the developmental performance of students as they develop literacy proficiency in a digital environment (Eyal, 2012; Leu, Kulikowich et al., 2013).

This means that literacy assessment in the online/digital environment may be able to expand the measurement components and focus of the assessment found in traditional school-based assessment programs and systems. In this literacy assessment environment, students continue to take quantitative, standardized, large-scale assessments that help to determine a student's strength of performance against grade-level standards that are useful in international and national literacy proficiency comparisons.

However, of equal importance, the digital environment includes qualitative assessments that help capture the stage of development and nature of the processing of the students as they move along a continuum of acquiring literacy proficiency in the online/digital environment. With advances in technology, it may be possible and easier to evaluate all types of student responses and work in these newer formats. Once assessments help to determine this type of performance, the information can be used directly to improve instruction and to support individual student growth. This development extends the work of informal inventories considerably.

Traditional standardized-based literacy assessments are still present at both international and national levels in the form of NAEP, PISA, and PIRLS. There is a rise in qualitative assessments to enhance the profiles of literacy proficiency in students in group and individual formats. Work at UCONN has explored the uses of qualitative assessment measures such as digital video recording all online reading actions that students experience while engaged in reading in the online environment as well as recording verbal think-aloud data to complete the assessment picture (Leu et al., 2008). At the international level, the G20 countries and the ITU are exploring self-assessments for determining progress, too (Coward et al., 2020; Chetty, 2017).

Moving in this direction for assessment may mean that mathematical models used in the past must be adapted to accommodate these changes in assessment.

THEME 4: LITERACY ASSESSMENT IS EVOLUTIONARY IN NATURE

Theme four is that literacy assessment is evolutionary in nature. It is currently evolving in four areas. First, it is evolving with technology as technology advances. Second, it is evolving with the reading tasks in the digital environment and with literacy processing theories. Third, it is evolving in the understanding of the strategies employed to construct meaning in the digital environment. Fourth, it is evolving in the ways assessment tasks measure literacy proficiency (Castek & Coiro, 2015).

Literacy assessment is evolving as technology offers ways to simulate online reading tasks that model what students are engaged in as part of their regular literacy curriculum. Technology also offers ways to support schools to engage in qualitative assessment by presenting ways to organize and present student project-based work and help to capture and present student project-based activities. As technology moves forward, assessment measures may have to move forward exponentially—no small task.

As literacy tasks and literacy processing theories develop for the digital environment, technology offers ways to create assessment tasks that mirror the developing understanding of how students construct meaning in the digital environment for real-life requirements. By evolving in these ways, literacy assessment stays current with both theory and practice for examining the changes in how we may be reading in the future.

Literacy assessments in the digital age are evolving as technological advances occur and inform us about the strategies students use to construct meaning successfully in a digital world. Large-scale international assessments such as PISA (2007) and PIRLS (2016) have moved to include simulated online environment literacy tasks. At the national level, NAEP moved to a digitally based literacy assessment in 2017 and is developing its new literacy assessment framework for 2026 to include literacy tasks that simulate reading in an online environment (US DOE, 2021). These measures should help identify strategies for attaining literacy proficiency.

Finally, researchers are exploring how technology can capture processing through better formats for assessment in online literacy tasks (Leu et al., 2008). Doing so can enhance our understanding of what can and cannot be measured now with the hope of hinting at what lies ahead for assessment measures.

THEME 5: TECHNOLOGY IN LITERACY ASSESSMENT CAN HELP COUNTER LOW SES AND DISABILITIES

Theme 5 is that literacy assessment uses technology to help counter the effects of low socioeconomic (SES) circumstances and disabilities (Balajthy, 2007; US Dept of Ed, 2021). This technological development will help SES students enter the literacy tasks to compensate for differing background knowledge and language skills than students in higher SES areas. The technology can provide helpful background knowledge for different or unfamiliar topics and vocabulary support.

These supports can help students engage more easily in the processing tasks of constructing meaning in the online/digital environment. Students with disabilities can be helped in this way, too, or with varying formats for presenting text so they can process it. The 2026 NAEP framework is working on using technology-based design tools that will give background knowledge, vocabulary explanations for little-used words, and motivational prompts to help students who may be disadvantaged along these lines.

All four ways that technology can enhance our work will help level the playing field for many kinds of students who otherwise may not perform well in the present test environment and be better prepared for the future of the evolving concept of literacy proficiency.

The concern that runs through past efforts at assessment and all of the themes presented here still raises central questions, such as "Is the reading process for constructing meaning changing in a digital world? If so, how so?" and "What are the implications of the emerging changes?"

Our hunch is that the reading process is changing and that further research efforts may wish to add several dimensions to the work. The first is a concern for generational differences in the reading process that may be influenced by exposure and openness to the technologies that continue to develop exponentially. The second is a concern for changes over time that can be studied in longitudinal research. A third concern is what other disciplines, such as neuroscience and its influences on learning processes, can do to shed light on the questions. These hunches are just that and a bit beyond the scope of this book.

However, the themes that we have identified here can guide further research to address these questions and transform our present knowledge both theoretically and practically with regard to various aspects of the reading process, the functioning of diverse readers, and the role of instruction and assessment for all readers. The hope is to broaden views on these concerns.

We hope that in the next part of this chapter, we can suggest ways to think further about assessment based on what we have said throughout this book. Perhaps we can suggest responses to questions with principles underlying a potential model for assessment and with examples of assessment tasks that reflect what we have said or are suggesting in this book.

PRINCIPLES FOR ASSESSMENT

Our discussions on assessment and instruction have given us a good background for projecting what we need to consider in broadening our view on what to aim for when assessing literacy proficiency, given its evolving nature. To accomplish our goal, we hope to present several key principles for assessment that reflect the theme-oriented presentation we suggested in the first section of this chapter.

The plan is to present several principles that we think are useful for anyone developing assessment models or tools for research or instruction. The principles that we suggest follow here in figure 4.3.

Principles for Assessment

1) Integrate Instruction and Assessment
2) Assess Evaluative Processing and Understanding
3) Distribute Assessment Period Over Time
4) Navigate Delivery Systems
5) Include Variation In Text Topic and Structure
6) Address the Developmental Level and Variation in Learner Background
7) Evaluate Learners' Responses to Assessment Tasks
8) Address the Learners' Ability to Develop Tasks Independently to Demonstrate Proficiency

---

Figure 4.3   Principles for Assessment.

Integrate Instruction and Assessment

First, it is clear to us that instruction and assessment must be integrated so that what is done in the classroom regularly is reflected in any tools we use to measure learner success. By doing this integration, we wish to reduce the end-of-the-year emphasis on test practice to determine performance. With this integration, assessment should show how well we have met the nature of instruction that we have proposed throughout this book and be a natural outgrowth of that instruction. This means extending and transforming past assessment measures to reflect more "real-world" needs as we move further into the digital world.

To accomplish this goal, examples from the chapter on instruction can be adapted as measures for assessment of the learner's response and can be evaluated for accomplishing the goal.

Assess Evaluative Processing and Understanding

Second, we need to assess (a) evaluative processing and understanding of all forms of messages—traditional or digital and (b) evaluate messaging and technological skills that have emerged and will continue to appear as time goes forward. This will give a measure of higher level thinking and understanding. Assessment tasks and items should be derived from the twenty characteristics in Chapter 1 and discussions in Chapter 2.

Attending to this second principle will also give us insight into the mental processing of messages as well as see if the learner has the skill to work independently and reason away from explicit text. This will move our knowledge forward for both assessments for research as well as for instruction.

Distribute Assessment Period over Time

Third, the assessment times for various developmental stages must be distributed over the year and show incremental growth. This means that different types of proficiency will be measured throughout the year rather than simply the same pre–post measures used presently. The assessment will also be used differently at different developmental levels from what is often used. That is, at first, third, and high school levels. We suggest starting assessment at grade 2, moving to grade 5, and then high school and adult levels. We think that this gives students time to consolidate abilities and time to introduce various assessment tasks appropriate for each level.

Navigate Delivery Systems

Fourth, learners must learn to navigate exponentially increasing delivery systems via multiple technological devices to access, evaluate, and integrate information and multiple messages. This means adapting to a variety of formats and the use of language. The digital messages in real-world texts will vary dramatically from traditional linear text and require greater flexibility to navigate. There may be a need for more recursive processing of text.

Include Variation in Text Topic and Structure

Fifth, as part of navigating delivery systems in assessment, we need to consider variations in topics and structure for familiarity and complexity in light of the learner's perceptions and abilities. We believe this knowledge helps us determine a learner's interest and motivation to persist in reading difficult or unfamiliar texts.

Address the Developmental Level and Variation in Learner Background

Sixth, we need to consider the developmental level of the learner along with the diversity in the backgrounds of different groups of learners. This will require a way to know more about the background by the knowledge learners have about text topics. Research in reading has shown background knowledge is a primary contributor to comprehension. We also think that shifting to second and fifth grade and eleventh grade better matches shifts in development.

We need to identify where learners are in their progression of skill, both traditional and technological. To do so, it may be helpful to determine the learner's perception of the ease of difficulty of the types of text used in the assessment. So, the inclusion of self-assessment measures will be helpful.

Evaluate Learners' Responses to Assessment Tasks

Seventh, the broadening view of the assessment of literacy will need to give us ways to evaluate the learner's responses during instruction as well as in our end goals of literacy proficiency that go beyond responses to multiple choice formats. When multiple-choice formats are used, they must tap evaluation of text rather than just literal or simple inference understanding. Various methods must be used to accomplish this task. Perhaps students can explain the reasons for their responses in self-assessment measures of digital text skills and the difficulty of the content in assessment tasks.

Further, assessment tools must give reliable ways to provide comparative and diagnostic information about this expanding nature of proficiency. Advances in technology may help to achieve this goal by supporting varied scoring systems beyond the multiple-choice format. Here is where qualitative measures may be useful and necessary.

ADDRESS THE LEARNERS' ABILITY TO DEVELOP TASKS TO DEMONSTRATE PROFICIENCY

Eighth, these assessment tools need to ask learners to show their ability to develop the type of tasks that we use to demonstrate literacy proficiency. This will force them to show how well they have integrated all of the skills they have learned to show how they will function in real-world situations. Learners will need to show how well they can create work to demonstrate that they can mirror the type of instruction they have received.

In sum, short passages on familiar narratives or simple expositions may not be adequate. Only multiple-choice responses to literal and simple text-based inferences will not give a complete picture of the literacy proficiency needed in the future. The testing industry must revamp its present instruments to meet these needs. Some of these principles are already emerging through the work we have reviewed. It must move forward into the everyday assessment of literacy proficiency that is part of a digital world and be flexible enough for the continuous changes to come.

MULTIDIMENSIONAL PLAN FOR EVALUATING LITERACY PROFICIENCY

The following multidimensional plan presents a timeline and the content for evaluating progress in achieving literacy proficiency. The plan integrates the ideas for the evolving concept of literacy and evaluation, media literacy and instruction, as well as what we have synthesized about the present state of activity on assessment. To accomplish this goal, the plan rests upon varied forms of evaluation for five different developmental levels at scheduled times for the assessment.

The plan considers some of what has been done in the past, along with changes we are predicting and proposing for the future. It integrates as best we can do the changes that we see based upon what we already have presented. The primary goal here is to shift the thinking from just pre–post comparative assessment to ongoing progressive evaluation that will better integrate instruction and assessment and broaden our view of what constitutes literacy proficiency.

What follows here is a visual (figure 4.4) of the plan, along with a description of the visual that illustrates the structure of the plan. The Part A chart (figure 4.4) of the visual illustrates the multilevel, multidimensional plan for achieving literacy proficiency. The Part B chart (figure 4.5) of the visual identifies specific tasks for assessing the types of literacy activities identified in the Part A visual. The Part B chart (figure 4.5) also suggests possible scoring schemes for those assessment tasks.

In Chart B (figure 4.5), we identify the tasks such as web pages and portfolios, and what the student needs to do to show literacy proficiency.

The assessment tasks are given by level and grade.

A generic framework for rubric scoring and self-assessment scales follows the text description of Visual A (figure 4.4) and Chart B (figure 4.5). A verbal description of Visual A (figure 4.4) and Chart B (figure 4.5) follows here.

Description of Part A Visual (figure 4.4) and Part B Chart (figure 4.5) on Multilevel Multidimensional Plan

The Part A Visual (figure 4.4) above depicts a multilevel, multidimensional plan for evaluating an ongoing process for achieving literacy proficiency at multiple points of development from beginning through proficiency. The plan can be used for classroom, school, district, regional, national, or international levels of assessment. It can remain the same with some reasonable adjustments for special or diverse populations.

Multidimensional Progress Plan

Model

Timetable + Substance: Format, Content, Learner Pereception, Scoring (Accommodations)

	November	Mid-Year	May	
LEVEL I 2nd grade	Basic Comprehension Text-Based Inferences		Text-Based Inferences Technical Skills (Computer-Aided)	**Learner Perception/ Self-Assessment**
LEVEL II 5th grade	Evaluative Literacy	Portfolio Progress Report	Evaluative Literacy Technical Skills (Digital)	
LEVEL III 11th grade	Evaluative Literacy Technical Skills (Digital)	Portfolio Progress Report	Integrated Work Portfolio	
LEVEL IV Post Adolescence/ Adult	FOCUS } Life Skills	Context Societal Workplace Everyday		
LEVEL V Expert Professional Development	The activities in LEVEL V can vary depending on the types of situations where PD is being carried out, and the needs of the participating educators. It should, however, reflect the principles and strategies described in Chapter Five.			

Evaluating performance at every level can be quantitative and qualitative in nature to allow both group comparison and individual assessment.

Learner Perception is a self-assessment of reaching literacy proficiency on measures of content and technical-related skills.

Figure 4.4   Multidimensional Progress Plan.

The Part A visual (figure 4.4) and the Part B (figure 4.5) chart represent the timeline and the substance of the assessment in terms of the format, the content, the learner/examinee's perception, and the scoring schemes and performance. The timeline allows ample time for appropriate instruction and consolidation of the abilities being developed. The Part B chart (figure 4.5) following the Part A (figure 4.4) visual and its description suggests sample assessment tasks and a generic scoring scheme.

Within developmental contexts, the developmental Levels I–V can correspond to multilevels of general development or diversity in the groups or individuals being assessed because it can be used in most environments either inside or outside of formal school grade contexts reasonably well. Within K-12 contexts, the development levels can correspond to graduated grade levels from grade 2 through adult proficiency. A final development level can be used for depicting expert proficiency that applies to training or troubleshooting. The substance of the final level is suggested in Chapter 5 on professional development.

Beyond the five levels is a scale for evaluating learner proficiency on measures of content and technical skills related to the activities related to all five levels.

The types of assessment proposed on the rubric and self-assessment give quantitative and qualitative measures of a broadened view of literacy proficiency.

ASSESSMENT LEVELS

Beginning Assessment—Developmental Level I or Grade 2

In terms of the timeline, we believe that formal assessment, when used with corresponding grade levels, can begin at the beginning of grade 2 or Developmental Level I, giving the learner the time needed to acquire and consolidate basic comprehension and text-based inferencing. Regarding Developmental Level I, for a general developmental level, it can simply be a starting point for assessment for anyone with beginning literacy proficiency. Starting here should give the learner time to experience narrative text and familiar topics. The focus is on basic comprehension and text-based inferences. Self-assessment of ability can begin in May to give insight into how the learner sees their ability to understand or do the task.

As the year progresses, instruction can focus on developing text-based inferences and technical skills, such as computer-aided work at a basic level. Assessment from November to May should show some individual growth and also allow for group comparison.

Figure 4.5 Chart B-Multidimensional Progress Plan: Sample Assessment Tasks

	November	Mid-Year	May
Level I-Second Grade	**Assessment Task: Teacher Created Simulated Web Page** Ex-Simulated web page of Life on a Farm -The web page has text/pictures/audio that describe what you find on a farm and what farmers do on a farm, that is, animals, buildings, growing crops -The web page has multiple links for the students to follow to read about what life is like on the farm <u>Basic comprehension questions:</u> (multiple choice or short answer) (1) Refer to different web pages—If you visited a farm, what would you find on the farm? (multiple choice or short answer) (2) What is the barn used for? (multiple choice or short answer) (3) Describe how the farmer grows crops? (short answer) <u>Scales:</u> rubric scoring -multiple-choice questions -rubrics (3 pts) for short-answer descriptive questions <u>Inference Questions:</u> (short answer) -Using the information found on the web pages: (1) Why does the farmer like showing school groups the farm? (2) How do you think visiting a farm helps kids understand where food comes from? <u>Scales:</u> rubric scoring -rubrics (3–5 pts) for short-answer inference questions		**Assessment Task: Teacher Created Simulated Web Page** Ex-Simulated web page of Pets -The web page has text/pictures/audio that describe Pets- common pets at home, taking care of pets, service pets/therapy pets -The web page has multiple links for the students to follow to read about pets <u>Inference Questions:</u> (short answer) -Using the information found on the web pages: (1) How would you convince your parents that your family should get a pet? (2) Do you think that service/therapy pets like being service/therapy animals? <u>Scales:</u> rubric scoring -rubrics (3–5 pts) for short-answer inference questions **Assessment Task: Technical Skills** -ex Navigating a web page -skills and strategies needed for locating information on a web page -Student self-assessment of the skills used for navigating a web page to locate information <u>Scale:</u> -self-assessment rating scale of the navigating tasks, that is, a list of skills and strategies that could be rated on a 1–5 scale of proficiency/ease of use

(continued)

Figure 4.5 (Continued)

	November	Mid-Year	May
Level II- Fifth Grade	**Assessment Task: Teacher Created Simulated Web Page**	**Assessment Task: Portfolio-Progress Report**	**Assessment Task: Teacher Created Simulated Web Page**

November:

Ex-Simulated web page of World Cultures
- The web page has text/pictures/audio that describe different countries/cultures around the world
- The web page has multiple links for the students to follow to read about different countries and cultures, that is, what people eat, how they dress, their holidays they celebrate, type of government, arts, schools, etc.

Evaluative Literacy Questions (open response)
(1) Refer to different web pages
- For students to learn about different cultures/countries, were these web pages helpful?
- What parts of the web pages were helpful?
- What other parts should be included?

Scales: rubric scoring
-rubrics for open-response questions

Mid-Year:

1) Students create a photo essay of their town and local area
2) Students create a portfolio demonstrating the development of comprehension strategies when reading in an online/digital environment
-skills/strategies covered in the portfolio could include:
-synthesizing information from multiple websites
-collaborating with other students to create summaries/syntheses while reading in an online/digital environment
-Evaluating the simulated websites

Portfolio Tasks:
(1) Create a photo essay that describes and promotes their town and area to tourists who are visiting the area

Scale: rubric scoring
2) Synthesis of information from the world cultures simulated web pages across multiple pages

Scale: rubric scoring
(3) Collaborating with a partner to add a new topic to the simulated web page of world cultures

Scale: rubric scoring
(4) Evaluating what could be added to the simulated web page to make it more helpful to a reader

Scale: rubric scoring

May:

Ex-Simulated web page Life in the Students' Community
- The web page has text/pictures/audio that describes what life is like in the students' community
- The web page has multiple links for the students to follow to read about life in their community-what, the important jobs are, what government is like, the layout of their town/city, the relationship of geography to their community

Evaluative Literacy Questions (open response)
(1) Refer to different web pages
- What makes their community a good place to live?
- What information on the website was helpful?
- What information needs to be added to the website?
- Are the people who wrote the website good to believe- to be listened to?
- What makes a person making a website credible? Someone to listen to?

Scales: rubric scoring
-rubrics for open-response questions

Assessment Task: Technical Skills
-ex Navigating and evaluating websites
-skills and strategies needed for locating information on a web page and evaluating web pages
-Student self-assessment of the skills used for navigating a web page to locate information and evaluating web pages for credibility

Level III- Eleventh Grade	Assessment Task: Teacher Created Simulated Web Page	Assessment Task: Portfolio-Progress Report	Assessment Task: Integrated Work Portfolio
	Ex-Simulated web page of the USA Government System -The web page has text/pictures/audio that describes the US government system -The web page has multiple links for the students to follow to read about the elements of the US governmental system- elections, parties, parts of government, history of democracy in the United States, etc. Evaluative Literacy Questions (open response) (1) Refer to different web pages -For students to learn about the US governmental system, were these web pages helpful? -What parts of the web pages were helpful? -What other parts should be included? Scales: rubric scoring -rubrics for open-response and short-answer questions Assessment Task: Technical Skills -ex Navigating and evaluating websites -skills and strategies needed for locating information on a web page and evaluating web pages -Student self-assessment of the skills used for navigating a web page to locate information and evaluating web pages for credibility	(1) Students create a Public Service Announcement (PSA) in a multimedia format on a current topic for the school or the community (2) Students create a podcast of a children's or young adult book for a younger audience to listen to. (3) Students create a simulated web page on a topic of their choice (4) Along with the website that they create, the students develop learning activities for younger grade-level students of learning activities that will develop online/digital comprehension strategies that the younger students can use while reading/engaging with the student-created website (5) Students create a portfolio demonstrating the development of comprehension strategies when reading in an online/digital environment -skills/strategies covered in the portfolio could include:	Scale: -self-assessment rating scale of the navigating tasks, that is, a list of skills and strategies that could be rated on a 1–5 scale of proficiency/ease of use -Self-assessment on a rating scale of the tasks involved in evaluating a website for credibility, that is, how proficient does the student think they are on the tasks involved in evaluating a web site **Assessment Task: Integrated Work Portfolio** (1) Students create a multimedia, interactive magazine or newspaper article similar to the NYT *Snowfall* article on the topic of their choice. (2) Students create a simulated Google site web page on a topic of their choice (3) Along with the website that they create, the students develop learning activities for a younger grade-level student of learning activities that will develop online/digital comprehension strategies that the younger students can use while reading/engaging with the student-created website (4) Students create a portfolio demonstrating the development of comprehension strategies when reading in an online/digital environment -skills/strategies covered in the portfolio could include: -synthesizing information from multiple websites -collaborating with other students to create summaries/syntheses while reading in an online/digital environment

(continued)

Figure 4.5 (Continued)

November	Mid-Year	May
Scale: -Self-assessment rating scale of the navigating tasks, that is, a list of skills and strategies that could be rated on a 1–5 scale of proficiency/ease of use -Self-assessment on a rating scale of the tasks involved in evaluating a website for credibility, that is, how proficient does the student think he/she is on the tasks involved in evaluating a website -Self-assessment- list of leveled descriptive categories of navigation and assessment skills becoming increasingly more complex -Students self-assess where they think that they fall on the scale of the categories describing the navigation and evaluation skills	-synthesizing information from multiple websites -collaborating with other students to create summaries/syntheses while reading in an online/digital environment -Evaluating the simulated websites Portfolio Tasks: (1) Public Service Announcement (PSA) on a current school or community topic Scale: rubric scoring (2) Podcast of a children's or young adult book for a younger audience to listen to. Scale: rubric scoring (3) Student creating a simulated website Scale: rubric scoring (4) Student-created instructional activities to develop comprehension strategies/processes for online/ digital reading Scale: rubric scoring (5) Synthesizing information from multiple websites Scale: rubric scoring (6) Collaborating with a partner to add a new topic to the simulated web page Scale: rubric scoring (7) Evaluating what could be added to the simulated web page to make it more helpful to a reader Scale: rubric scoring	-Evaluating the simulated websites Portfolio Tasks: (1) Student-created multimedia news or magazine-type article Scale: rubric scoring (2) Student creating a simulated website Scale: rubric scoring (3) Student-created instructional activities to develop comprehension strategies/ processes for online/digital reading Scale: rubric scoring (4) Synthesizing information from multiple websites Scale: rubric scoring (5) Collaborating with a partner to add a new topic to the simulated web page Scale: rubric scoring (6) Evaluating what could be added to the simulated web page to make it more helpful to a reader Scale: rubric scoring

Level IV-
Societal
Environment
-Adult

Life Skills

(1) Societal

(a) Create an Instagram Carousel of a current community topic that could be shared on the town's or cities website/Facebook page or other media presence

(b) Self-created website on a current cultural/societal topic

(2) Workplace

(a) Create a screencast demonstrating how to do something connected to work that could be shared with fellow workers.

(b) Create a blog tracing the history/evolution of a topic in their workplace/profession

(3) Everyday/Personal

(a) Create an audio travel documentary of describing a trip taken

(b) Create a website that investigates a topic of their choice, that is, something that they are curious about, and share the website with friends

Evaluation Scales

(1) Rubrics

(2) Self-evaluation scale

Intermediate Assessment – Development Level II or Grade 5

Moving from Development Level I takes us to grade 5 and Developmental Level II, where the assessment of ability in November takes the form of evaluative literacy. Here assessment begins to evaluate some of the twenty characteristics of evaluative literacy that we presented in Chapters 1 and 2. Developmentally, the learner is ready to move beyond text-based inferences to make reflective judgments about narrative and expository texts. Website work requires greater navigational skills. Self-assessment of the difficulty of the task continues.

Critical thinking is at the center of literacy proficiency here, and the learner's abilities move beyond basic comprehension and simple technical skills, reflecting the move into the digital world while maintaining traditional literacy proficiency. The assessment in May adds the advancing technical skills required in the digital world, as we described in Chapter 2. This year-end assessment has given the learners the time needed to consolidate their abilities.

Here, the format for assessment tasks changes from multiple-choice or short answer to a variety of assessment formats. Here, we also see a mid-year progress report form of a portfolio that requires more difficult skills from the learner. The Part B chart (figure 4.5) that follows the description of the levels addresses this variety of assessment formats.

Post-Intermediate Assessment— Development Level III or Grade 11

Developmental Level III assessment is delayed until grade 11 or a developmental level that approximates this grade to give time for further development of cognition and abilities enhanced through broadened instructional practices, as seen in Chapters 2 and 3. Almost eliminated are the simple multiple-choice or short-answer formats to reflect the shift to the evaluation of the twenty characteristics described earlier in the book. The difficulty of the text formats shifts further to include argumentative structure and less familiar topics. Again, a portfolio at mid-year assesses ongoing progress.

Technical skills have multiplied considerably beyond simply using basic navigational skills to integrating evaluation and digital abilities into project-type assessment reflecting category two and three instructional tasks described in Chapter 3 on instruction. Work is presented in a more formal portfolio form, including a variety of assessment tasks. The mid-year progress report begins to reflect this change.

Adult —Developmental Level IV or Life Skills

Developmental Level IV Adulthood focuses on Life Skills needed to function in a larger society than school, home, and immediate environments. It means having the ability to function in all aspects of society, such as the day-to-day requirements of traditional paper-based communication as well as digital-based tasks such as using credit cards, mobile phones, banking, shopping, or voting. It means carrying out workplace requirements and tasks, many of which require critical thinking and communication for problem-solving.

To assess these abilities, we need a variety of assessment tasks that are more like what is carried out on a day-to-day basis, along with those requiring longer sustaining of efforts. Many require a high level of independent functioning as well as collaborative work. Scoring schemes for all levels shift to integrated formats. We see greater use of portfolios and project tasks. Assessing those abilities requires a broadened view of what constitutes literacy proficiency.

Expert—Level V Assessment

There also may be a Level V Expert category for assessment that involves much of what we will discuss in Chapter 5 on professional development. This will be on training and troubleshooting. The activities in Level V can vary depending on the situations where professional development is being carried out and the needs of the participating educators. It should, however, reflect the principles and strategies described in Chapter 5.

With a sense of the substance of each level in mind, we move to assessment formats and scoring schemes that represent ways to evaluate literacy proficiency.

ASSESSMENT FORMATS AND SCORING SCHEMES

Many tests in development still have had to confine themselves to binary and Likert-type scale ratings for measurement purposes. However, testing endeavors such as PIRLS and NAEP, and we are guessing test publishing houses, are working to identify assessment tasks that broaden our views on literacy proficiency as we move into digital environments. Although they still have constraints in measurement that keep them focused on simple scoring schemes for evaluating work that correlates well between computer and human scoring for m-c and open response type items, they still need to move toward additional types of test-type items.

We guess that as time progresses, so will these testing endeavors to move beyond m-c and simple open response type items. We hope to direct thinking and formal assessment to the varied instructional and assessment tasks that we have identified in Chapter 3 and in Chart B (figure 4.5) as ones that are coming now and into the future. We are looking to find ways to evaluate more integrated tasks that are coming from the digital world.

Scoring schemes for the type of assessment tasks identified in Chart B (figure 4.5) are variable depending upon the task and the degree of proficiency needed to be considered successful. Multiple-choice and open-response items still are the ones used most often. Often, too, the existing rubrics used in several settings vary in generality and detailed descriptions of the components of the categories within a rubric depending upon the specific assessment task being evaluated. Individual tasks and portfolio schemes take different forms but do have some overlap. Integrated tasks require multidimensional schemes similar to portfolios.

What we hope to do in this section on scoring schemes is to direct our thinking to ways to incorporate these variations into ways to evaluate student work in either informal or formal ways. To accomplish this goal, we simply will illustrate and reference tasks that coordinate with the levels of proficiency in the multidimensional plan that we presented in Visual A (figure 4.4).

The most basic scoring scheme still is the multiple-choice format used to assess basic comprehension and simple inference. What is emerging now is an open-response scoring scheme and rubric evaluation. Their use is described here.

OPEN-RESPONSE SCORING AND
LARGE-SCALE ASSESSMENTS

Open-response questions on large-scale reading assessments are scored on rubric scales of varying length. The PIRLS assessment used a two-point scoring scale in the 2016 administration of the PIRLS assessment and a three-point scale in the 2021 administration of the assessment. On the 2016—0–2 scale, a 2 represents complete comprehension, 1 represents partial comprehension, and 0 represents no comprehension (Mullis & Martin, 2019; Wry & Mullis, 2023; Martin et al., 2015).

The NAEP assessment also uses two scoring scales depending on the complexity of the questions (Nations Report Card, 2023). The simpler type of question —a short constructed response (SCR) questions are scored on a three-level —0–2 scale (2 – full comprehension, 1 – partial comprehension, and 0 —little or no comprehension). The more complex open-response questions-extended constructed responses (ECR) are scored on a four-level—0–3 scale, with 3 representing an extensive answer, 2 representing an essential answer, 1 representing a partial answer, and 0 representing an unsatisfactory answer.

The Partnership for Assessment of Readiness for College and Carers (PARCC) assessments expanded the open-response scoring scale to five levels (1–5) (New Meridian Resource Center, 2023). At each level, the response is scored on the accuracy of analysis, use of evidence, and organization. When the PARCC assessment framework was implemented at the state level, some states used the five-point scale while others, such as Massachusetts, expanded the scale to include a more gradated review of the written response on a six-point scale (0–6) (DESE MCAS, 2023).

RUBRIC CATEGORIES

A review of the Assessments and Rubrics page of a popular educational website (Schrock, 2023) found over 150 rubrics listed for curriculum topic areas and instructional projects. In general, in the literacy and digital/media literacy areas, the rubrics seem to cluster around products produced in six main areas:

1) Social communication
   - Discussion boards, Twitter, etc.
2) Multimedia presentations
3) Audio presentations
   - podcasts
4) Visual Presentations (primarily)
   - Instagram, etc.
5) Written Presentations(primarily)
   - blogs, etc.
6) Digital Portfolios

Some of These Types of Projects Have Been Identified in Chart B (figure 4.5).

However, in general, the rubrics for digital literacy/multimedia tasks have four to five levels of performance categories across the top of the rubric and 1-n elements of the task down the side of the rubric. The rubrics vary from this general format depending on the complexity of the task being scored and the purpose of the assessment.

What we wish to suggest is a sample generic rubric framework to be used with both individual assessment tasks and project-type tasks such as portfolios. A sample framework follows here (figure 4.6).

Table 4.6   Sample Generic Framework for Tasks or Project in Rubric Form for Digital Literacy/Multimedia Tasks Proficiency

Elements of Task or Project	Needs Instruction 1pt	Emerging 2pts	Develop- ing 3pts	Proficient 4pts	Exemp lary 5pts	Total per Task
Element #1						
Element #2						
Element #3						
Element #4						
Element #5						
Element #n						
Range of possible points	0-5	0-10	0-15	0-20	0-25	Total Score (0-25pts)

Figure 4.7   Self-Assessment and Scoring Scale—Content

| | | Can Do with | | |
| | Easy | Help | Too Difficult | |
Content	(3 pt)	(2 pts)	(1 pts)	Points Across
Vocabulary				
Sentences				
Organization of ideas				
Familiarity of topic				
Difficulty with reading to understand				
Interest in topic				
				Total Points

Figure 4.8   Self-Assessment and Scoring Scale—Technical Skills

| | | Can Do with | | |
| | Easy | Help | Too Difficult | Points |
Technical Skills	(3 pt)	(2 pts)	(1 pts)	Across
Clarity of directions to complete the task				
Following links to sites				
Familiar with technical terms				
Create digital work				
Followed presentation of content				
				Total Points

Your thoughts about taking the test

This generic rubric can be used at all levels of instruction or assessment of literacy proficiency. The boxes across the rubric grid would contain descriptions of what a task or project element would look like at that level. The term task applies to items such as podcasts, blogs, etc. The term project applies to portfolios and integrated work that combine digital and traditional work. The total score can be used to make comparisons across groups and individuals.

In addition to the generic rubric form for evaluating tasks and projects, we need a scoring scale for evaluating a learner's perception of their literacy proficiency in the form of a self-assessment scoring scale.

SELF-ASSESSMENT OF SKILLS SCORING SCHEME

In addition to the generic framework just described, we would like to present a self-assessment scoring scale. There are two parts to the substance of the self-assessment scoring scale that can be used to determine the learner's perception of their sense of ability in completing any assessment task administered. The scoring scale considers the learner's interaction with the content of the task as well as the ability of technical skills to navigate or create the tasks. The self-assessment is administered during the spring assessment for all levels. The test administrator may guide the second-grade level learners through the assessment.

The following text can be used as directions to the learners. If necessary, the directions can be read to the learners for level one.

Directions to Learners

When you took this test of your thoughts about your ability to do the tasks, you had to do some things that made the work easy, needed help with doing, or found it too difficult to understand or navigate with all of the tasks. The two things are the content and the technical skills. In the chart, please put an X to show what you think about the work for content or technical skill. At the end of your work with the chart, write any other of your thoughts about taking the test.

The above sample generic rubric framework for rubrics and self-assessment scoring scale for literacy proficiency should guide those administering the test in evaluating a learner's literacy proficiency using quantitative and qualitative measures. Both instruments may be adapted for each test administered at each grade level.

We hope that we have made useful suggestions for a rubric and a self-assessment scoring scale that reflects what we have said in this book. We hope, too, that they are helpful at every level of assessing literacy proficiency as may exist in the future.

In sum, we have given you a reasonable timetable for measuring progress, examples of specific types of assessment tasks, as well as generic means for scoring schemes. We hope that our diverse suggestions and examples in this chapter move thinking on assessment activity forward and reflect our earlier thinking on all our literacy proficiency, evaluation, media concerns, and instruction with what we see happening with present and future efforts of literacy proficiency.

CHAPTER SUMMARY

This chapter presents where we are going with a change in how we evaluate and assess literacy proficiency as we move into a digital world. To accomplish this goal, we briefly trace previous literacy practices and then show a direction for change that includes several themes and principles to guide that change. We illustrate our suggestions with what we hope are useful models to generate future work.

PART III

PROFESSIONAL DEVELOPMENT

Chapter 5

Guiding Others in Developing Literacy Proficiency

OVERVIEW

This chapter addresses a primary concern and the crucial implications for implementing significant changes related to instruction and assessment of literacy proficiency. The chapter explores professional development as a means for influencing and implementing changes for achieving literacy proficiency.

The focus is on educating educators/providers on evaluative and media literacy and the technology needed and available for responding to various forms of text in a digital world. We then look at how this influences training learners and the general populace in achieving and demonstrating their success with achieving literacy proficiency. The chapter attempts to answer the question, "How do we achieve our goal of making a literate populace in a digital world?"

GUIDING QUESTIONS

What background knowledge on evaluative and media literacy and the influence of technology shape training procedures? How do we build this background?

How can we blend conceptual knowledge and practical hands-on skills?

Who are the individuals involved in professional development? What are their roles?

How do the developers' and the educators' perspectives differ from the learners'?

In what ways would "learning communities" serve as a model for professional development?

What might the possible benefits of "literacy coaches" be in supporting educator growth through professional development?

THE URGENCY OF EVALUATIVE LITERACY

At the core of this book is a commitment to raising the consciousness of learners, educators, parents, administrators, and all members of society to the critical importance of evaluative literacy. As our society becomes increasingly divided across race, nationality, income, gender, politics, and religion, the need for evaluative literacy increases, and educators assume an increasingly vital role. While the work of educators appears more daunting than ever, the belief in the power of transformational education remains steadfast.

Through the collaborative teaching and learning model embedded in evaluative literacy, learners gain experience and knowledge to become citizens who possess the qualities necessary for democracy: the ability to think and read critically across a broad spectrum of texts, the capacity to understand multiple perspectives and points of view, and the insight to envision the consequences that misleading, erroneous texts can have on human lives.

Evaluative literacy reflects an approach to teaching that involves empowering learners to engage in thinking that is thoughtful, nuanced, and critical. Given that so much public communication is notable for misinformation and disinformation, this challenge is substantial. Yet, through a recursive process of questioning and discovering, learners can become empowered to derive meaning from texts by developing an awareness of how language is used, as well as an awareness of varying perspectives.

This process is supported by the teaching of strategies constructed to provide learners with the necessary tools to work through texts and evaluate the messages. Embedded in this teaching and learning is the awareness that both traditional and digital text are forms of communication: digital text continues to be communication within a relatively new medium.

As the need for evaluative literacy increases, efforts must be made to identify processes to ensure that educators receive support as they strive to incorporate evaluative literacy strategies into their teaching. Often, when educational practices need to be changed or improved, one primary vehicle for change is professional development for educators.

PROFESSIONAL DEVELOPMENT AS
A VEHICLE FOR CHANGE

When educational practices need to be changed, consideration is given to professional development for educators. Although regarded as the primary means to achieve change and improvement, the results are often ineffective (Borko, 2004; Joyce & Showers, 2002; Lieberman & Miller, 2014; Rowell, 2007). Considering the important role professional development plays in educator education, the reasons why professional development is often deemed ineffective must be examined.

One reason attributed to the ineffectiveness of professional development has been the lack of support and lack of follow-through for continued support and learning for educators. According to Scot, Callahan, and Urquhart (2009), another reason that professional development has often been ineffective is that educators need ongoing professional development in a supportive environment and, ironically, the teaching environment itself is not supportive of change and is often a contributing factor to ineffective professional development.

Fullan (2014) goes so far as to describe the teaching environment as being stressful. This description offers insight into the environment created by the pressure educators face to improve test scores. It is not surprising that the pressure created by an overemphasis on testing leads to resistance by educators to resist embracing strategies that are not directly related to learners' test performances. Another obstacle to change, often cited, is the lack of leadership (Fullan, 2002; Sarason, 1990; Scot et al., 2009; Tallerico, 2014).

Finally, a growing body of evidence suggests that top-down mandates impede the progress of educational reform (Liberman & Miller, 2014; Giles & Hargreaves, 2006). Joyce and Showers (2002) concluded that this traditional demonstration-type staff development with no future follow-up has been largely ineffective; for these reasons, this model has been challenged by the growth-in-practice model of professional learning (Lieberman & Miller, 2014).

The following section examines a few effective growth-in-practice models of professional development to support improvement in teaching evaluative literacy.

THE IMPORTANCE OF TEACHER INQUIRY

In addition to identifying conditions that impede professional development, researchers have identified key elements of professional development that make change possible. One key factor in effective professional development is the importance of teacher inquiry. As teachers make decisions about their instructional practices, they continually examine and reflect on the effectiveness of their practices. Jacobs and Yendol-Hoppy (2014) point out that teacher inquiry focuses on the teacher's concerns.

When invested in an area of interest, teachers assume the stance of inquiry, formulate their questions, grapple with answers, determine possible solutions, and refine and ask more questions (Jacobs & Yendol-Hoppy 2014; Richardson & Placier, 2001). Teacher inquiry embodies a process for articulating ideas, collecting data, refining and redefining knowledge, and building on that knowledge to create new knowledge. This process is recursive in that "inquiry is nested within cycles of deliberate, self-regulated attempts to advance their own learning" (Butler & Schnellert, 2012, p. 1208). This recursive process lies at the heart of learning communities.

PROFESSIONAL LEARNING COMMUNITIES

One key element in creating an effective learning community is a school's commitment to collaboration through which educators, support staff, and administrators work together toward a common goal: "Teaching learning communities appear to be the most effective, practical method for changing day-to-day classroom practice" (Williams, 2007/2008, p. 39). Hackman (2002) further elaborates on the conditions for establishing an effective professional learning community.

The team must have both a compelling direction for its work and an enabling structure that supports teamwork. The team must also operate within a supportive organizational context. This shift from top-down professional development to professional learning communities represents a shift emphasizing collaboration and teamwork rather than an administrative imposition of teaching practices.

While the goals, objectives, and topics might vary from school to school, learning communities believe in creating an organizational structure that fosters collaboration and promotes collaborative inquiry (Lieberman & Miller, 2014). This model moves away from the training model of professional development, which relies predominantly on expert knowledge, toward a growth-in-practice model, which values educator knowledge and practice.

Learning communities emphasize the following practices: educators being involved in steady, intellectual work that promotes meaningful engagement over time; educators engaging in collaborative inquiry and incorporating their ideas into practice; educators drawing on their own experience and knowledge; and educators actively engaging in reflection, analysis, and critique (Lieberman & Miller, 2014). Professional learning communities have the potential to provide educators with the opportunities to engage in high-level thinking, paralleling the emphasis and practices for them to follow in their classes.

Five Shared Principles of Learning Communities

The theoretical underpinnings of much of the research on effective professional learning communities reflect five principles (Bauserman et al., 2014).

The first principle is grounded in the importance of educator agency. Professional development begins by engaging educators and results in the ownership, agency, and shared understanding of the professional development processes. In the context of professional learning, educator agency is the capacity of educators to act purposefully and constructively to direct their professional growth and contribute to the growth of their colleagues (Au, 2013; Johnson-Parsons, 2012).

The second principle is that professional development occurs over time as participants address meaningful problems of practice (e.g., integrating critical thinking and digital pedagogy, addressing evaluative literacy within a digital medium). This contrasts with a single professional development presentation model that purports that one or two sessions constitute the entire training and will result in a change and improvement to educator practices.

The third principle highlights the power of dialogue as a means for engaging in inquiry. Effective professional development creates various opportunities for dialogue among the members of the professional learning communities, allowing the educators time to delve into topics and experience sustained growth over time. The construction of meaning characterizes a dialogical approach and focuses on the needs of the participants.

The fourth principle is that professional development is systemic, involving all key participants. Systemic professional development creates a common purpose and shared responsibility for reaching concrete goals (e.g., developing lessons to teach evaluative literacy across grade levels explicitly). It uses a variety of settings, including whole school, department, and grade-level meetings, to provide opportunities for dialogue (Au & Raphael, 2011).

The fifth principle is that professional development is sustained (Darling-Hammond et al., 2009). This sustaining process involves alternating whole-group and small-group sessions and must be continued over a sufficiently long period of time for the goal to be accomplished. The more complex and ambitious the goal is, the more time must be dedicated to its accomplishment (Au, 2013).

Professional learning communities illustrate that educator involvement in creating knowledge, exploring ideas, listening, learning, reflecting with others, and contributing to change must be a significant part of effective professional learning and development.

LITERACY COACHES

Along with professional learning communities, the importance of coaching is advocated in the professional development literature (Griffith et al., 2014; Darling-Hammond & Sykes, 1999; Casey, 2006; Toll, 2018). Much of this research in the area of professional development embraces coaching and identifies five different kinds of support that can be provided to educators: discussion of theories, demonstration and modeling of lessons, opportunities in sessions and in classrooms to practice the newly learned strategies, feedback in the form of support and assistance from peers or supervisors and in-class coaching.

Cathy Toll (2018) continues to echo the need for collaboration, reflection, and partnership to achieve ongoing change. Consistent throughout the research is the belief that educators need to have opportunities to learn about strategies, observe the modeling of strategies and techniques, and practice and receive feedback on the strategies in their classrooms. Research supports the idea that educators need consistent practice in their classrooms for the desired strategies to become part of the educators' instructional strategies (Fullan, 1991; Hodges, 1996; Smylie, 1995). Research also emphasizes the need for the guidance of coaches working with educators (Lyons & Pinnell, 2001; Casey, 2006; Toll, 2018).

One important implication of this work is that for educators to integrate meaningful concepts and strategies into their teaching practices, this knowledge must be accompanied by opportunities for educators to observe the modeling of these strategies and to receive feedback while implementing them in their classrooms. A second implication in this research is that when the presentation of new concepts is accompanied by modeling and feedback, then change is possible.

While it is clear that professional learning communities and educational coaching have tremendous potential to lead to change and improvement in evaluative literacy, both models also emphasize the power of individual educators to apply the theories of evaluative literacy to teaching practices.

INDIVIDUAL EDUCATORS

Individual educators have tremendous power, and meaningful change depends on each educator's belief that improvement and change are possible. This book is rooted in a belief in the value of raising the awareness of learners and educators about the importance of evaluative literacy. Professional development models such as professional learning communities and educational coaching cite collaboration, reflection, dialogue, sustainability, and community as necessary elements to make changes and improvements in teaching.

The hope is that the ideas, lessons, and models in this book begin conversations, spark collaborative thinking, and create teaching and learning that have, at its core, evaluative literacy. The potential strength of evaluative literacy to impact the lives of learners lies in the power of individual educators to transform these theories into practices. Education is, in the words of Paulo Freire, an "inescapable concern." The need for evaluative literacy is part of that inescapable concern. As educators strive to educate the minds and hearts of learners, evaluative literacy must become a central part of the educational journey.

PROFESSIONAL DEVELOPMENT SPECIFIC TO MEDIA LITERACY AND PRODUCTION

As we move into teaching evaluative and media literacy in the digital age, learners are not alone in needing explicit instruction in both how to use and evaluate digital media. Each individual educator brings different experiences and skill sets to the classroom. With digital media and technology, the range of experiences and skills is vast. Because of this need, extensive professional development is needed to get educators on the same page. This can include instruction and hands-on practice with specific technology and media, as well as the evaluative skills and tools needed to analyze media messages.

Most educators have not taken media literacy courses as part of their educational experiences. For a long time, these courses were geared toward communication and media majors. However, the proliferation of media messages and expansion of digital media and technology necessitates media literacy become a staple in educator education. Educators must explore their relationship with and use of media and the biases and experiences they bring to evaluate media messages in the ways we have encouraged in this book.

When preparing professional development for educators, it is essential first to evaluate their background knowledge and prior experiences. Because some educators will be well versed in media production and technology, it's often a good idea to break professional development opportunities into smaller workshops focusing on specific tools and skills. For example, someone with no media or media literacy experience would benefit from direct instruction covering basic skills. Once they have mastered the basics, they could move on to more advanced workshops covering the integration of evaluative literacy in the digital age into their classroom practices and assessments.

Types of Professional Development for Media Literacy

As noted earlier in this chapter, there are many avenues of professional development, including in-service opportunities, workshops, seminars, conferences, courses, and professional learning communities. When thinking about how to structure professional development in both media and evaluative literacy, it is important to consider both the needs of the educators and the capability of internal professional development resources. Ideally, districts will provide professional development experiences at varying levels of skill development and via varied modalities to best reach all educators, regardless of their prior learning or understanding.

Workshops and seminars are traditional professional development methods in education and can be held at the school, district, or state level. Occasionally districts provide internal professional development and invite faculty and staff to share their expertise, but more often than not, these experiences are run by external entities who are invited into the schools by administrators. These experts provide an overview of a particular topic, providing attendees with a grounding in the subject matter and vocabulary, but generally shy away from specific instruction in media production tools.

Though traditionally, this method of professional development has been in person, the COVID-19 pandemic revealed the benefits of having these kinds of opportunities via Zoom or other online formats. The flexibility that comes with online options is unmatched. Furthermore, it allows educators to connect with peers worldwide, offering greater opportunities for networking and learning about how other districts are teaching media literacy and media production.

Conferences and symposiums are larger-scale professional development events that allow educators to interact with researchers and industry experts. They allow for greater networking opportunities and are usually held at the state, regional, national, or international levels. Participants have the opportunity to listen to keynote speakers and then can tailor their experiences through a choice of concurrent workshops.

This kind of professional development is wonderful for educators who have a grounding in media literacy and production and are looking to learn or improve specific skills. However, it is difficult for public school educators to get the funding and release time to participate in this professional development. It would behoove districts to allocate funding for educators who would benefit from attending conferences,

While courses are another effective form of professional development, they can be difficult to squeeze into a professional's packed schedule. However, the last few years have seen an improvement and increase in online courses and webinars that provide educators flexibility in pacing and location. Participants can learn asynchronously—completing the material from home and at their own pace.

Generally, courses and webinars are offered by outside organizations, including universities/colleges, professional organizations, and education nonprofits. They are excellent for deeper learning about a specific aspect of media literacy or for developing advanced media production skills.

Professional learning communities allow educators to learn from their peers in a supportive, school-based environment. When creating a community centered around improving media literacy and production skills, it might be helpful to include members of the student body as well. It is not uncommon for learners to develop media production skills outside of the classroom, including photography, audio/video production, website design, social media, and more. Including learners in the community allows educators the opportunity to learn from them, as well as provide a window into the tools they are using and the skills they have acquired.

CHALLENGES AND SOLUTIONS FOR PROFESSIONAL DEVELOPMENT IN MEDIA LITERACY

There is a wide range of challenges to professional development for educators, including limited time, lack of funding, irrelevance, lack of skills and/ or follow-up mentoring and support, resistance to change, lack of differentiation, inadequate networking and collaborative opportunities, and access and equity issues. Any one of these barriers makes it difficult for educators to acquire the knowledge, skills, and confidence they need to implement media literacy and production into their curriculum. Multiple barriers only increase the likelihood that educators will resist change and refuse to integrate these important skills and tools into their teaching.

Limited Time: It is often difficult for educators to integrate professional development into their practice, given the demands of today's teaching load coupled with personal and social commitments and responsibilities. Often, educators have limited time and resources, which can make it difficult to attend a conference or online course. One solution to this particular challenge is to offer professional development opportunities during the school day or to provide the time and funding for educators to attend conferences and symposiums.

Limited Funding: Professional development programming requires financial resources for organizing workshops, conferences, or acquiring instructional materials. Many school districts need to earmark more funding for professional development or simply need more funding to allocate. Limit funding can restrict the opportunities for educators to access professional development outside of the district and/or limit the availability of high-quality professional development opportunities offered in-house.

Relevance and Applicability: Ideally, professional development should align with the specific needs of the individual educator. If either the content or the format of professional development does not address an immediate concern or a perceived need, an educator may dismiss the opportunity as unhelpful or, at worst, a waste of time. The material must be relevant and applicable to their curriculum and provide tangible knowledge and skills that can be immediately implemented into their practice.

Lack of Skills and/or Follow-Up Mentoring and Support: One of the biggest barriers facing educators integrating media literacy and production into their curriculum is their perception that they need more expertise and support to teach these concepts and skills effectively. To address this challenge, schools or districts can provide direct support and training to help educators become confident in their media literacy skills and comfortable with media production skills and tools, such as creating podcasts and websites. This can include coaching and mentoring, online courses, in-service workshops, and professional learning communities.

However, it is important to note that continued support after professional development is essential for an educator to transfer their learning into their practice. Educators need access to experts within the school or district who can provide extended mentoring.

Though many districts have trained literacy coaches and mentors, they may need more skills in media literacy and production to be effective in this role. In this case, it is important that these folks also go through extensive professional development to provide adequate support to the faculty as they implement media literacy and production into their curriculum and practice. Too often, districts bring in outside organizations to provide a one-and-done workshop or professional development experience that leaves educators in a lurch when they need support over subsequent weeks and months.

Resistance to Change: Some educators may resist incorporating media literacy into their teaching practice for myriad reasons, including their perceived lack of knowledge/skill, a lack of understanding about the importance of media literacy, or a general fear of change. To overcome this challenge, schools/districts can provide in-service workshops and training to help educators develop their competencies, understand the benefits of media literacy, and provide guidance and mentoring on incorporating media literacy into existing curricula.

Examining the integration of technology for media production specifically, Etmer (1999) created The Barrier to Technology Integration model that examines those barriers that prevent educators from integrating technology into their instruction. He outlined two primary barriers—first-order (external) and second-order (internal). Whereas first-order barriers include school culture, professional development, access to technology, and factors outside an educator's locus of control, second-order barriers are internal, such as their likes/dislikes for particular tools or personal beliefs about integrating technology into the classroom.

Identifying which of these barriers prevents educators from incorporating media and technology into their curriculum and practice is crucial in determining the best options for professional development.

Lack of Differentiation: We understand that learners bring various prior knowledge and skill sets to the classroom. No two learners are alike in their abilities and needs. The same holds for educators—they have varied back-grounds, experiences, skills, and needs. Professional development opportunities that do not differentiate instruction to meet these individual needs may fail to engage or address the specific requirements of all participants. Because of this, it is important to scaffold and tailor professional development opportunities, particularly for media literacy and production skills that vary widely from individual to individual.

Scaffolding professional development is similar to the practice used by educators when breaking complex subject matter and assignments into smaller, more manageable chunks. To do so for media literacy and production includes providing educators with the support and resources they need to build their knowledge and skills gradually and sequentially. Some of the following strategies can be particularly helpful when building a professional development plan for media literacy and production:

Begin with the basics by introducing educators to the foundational concepts of media literacy. This should come before any attempt at media production. These core concepts are essential for understanding. As addressed in previous chapters, these foundational ideas include identifying the purpose and audience of media messages, analyzing media techniques, and understanding media bias. This foundational work can be done through workshops, seminars, or online courses and should be geared toward folks with little to no background in media and media literacy.

Once educators have a basic understanding of the concepts of media literacy, next, provide examples and model teaching strategies. Examples of lesson plans and student work can help them envision how media literacy can be integrated into the curriculum. Furthermore, it provides the opportunity for educators to observe media literacy lessons in the classroom. Although this can be done via videos, it is even more effective when part of a professional learning community, allowing educators to sit in on their peers' classrooms.

As educators begin integrating media literacy into their curriculum and practice, they offer opportunities for coaching and feedback. This is where mentoring becomes a crucial part of the process. Educators need feedback on their instruction and help to refine their skills. This can also allow mentors to provide educators with resources, including lesson plans, instructional materials, and assessment tools. These resources can be shared widely through online platforms, allowing mentors to work with several educators simultaneously and helping facilitate professional learning communities.

The more comfortable educators become, the more effectively they can collaborate with their peers. Educators should be encouraged and rewarded for sharing ideas and resources and providing feedback to their peers. As they become experts, they can begin to mentor educators in the beginning stages of integrating media literacy into the curriculum.

Additionally, at this point, they can begin developing their media production skills. They may learn how to create podcasts and then integrate that activity into their curriculum and practice. As they acquire media production skills, the scaffolding process remains the same—begin with the basics, provide examples and model teaching strategies, offer opportunities for coaching and feedback, share resources, and provide mentorship.

Inadequate Networking and Collaborative Opportunities: The opportunity to network with other educators integrating media literacy and production into their curriculum and practice is essential for professional development. Unfortunately, limited opportunities for peer interaction, collaboration, or networking make it difficult for educators to share ideas, experiences, and best practices.

Professional Learning Communities are one way to increase collaboration between educators in a school/district. Conferences and symposiums are also excellent avenues for this connection and support. However, schools/districts can also partner with local colleges/universities, professional organizations, or education nonprofits to provide their educators with access to experts in the field and learn from a diverse set of perspectives.

Access and Equity: Access to professional development opportunities in the United States varies widely by city, district, state, and region. They may also vary based on socioeconomic factors, community demographics, and district/government support. These issues are further compounded when we take into account access to technology. Not all schools/districts have equal access to the latest technology. This can hamper efforts to include media literacy and production in instruction and practice.

Ensuring equitable access to high-quality professional development and the latest technology and media production tools is crucial to avoid exacerbating existing educational disparities.

Addressing all of these challenges and barriers to professional development in media literacy and production requires adequate funding, careful planning, integrated support, and a commitment to meet the diverse needs of educators. Professional development programs should be flexible and relevant and incorporate differentiated instruction, scaffolding, mentoring, collaboration, and follow-up support. The school/district needs to establish a culture that values and prioritizes professional development.

The ideas presented in this chapter can be applied to many forms of professional development. We simply confined ourselves to evaluative and media literacy by presenting general concerns and illustrating those concerns to media literacy because of the pervasiveness of media in the growing need for evaluative literacy in a digital world.

CHAPTER SUMMARY

This chapter addresses challenges and principles for successful professional development by focusing on applying these principles through examples of media literacy and technology. What we propose are suggestions and not a step-by-step procedure for doing professional development.

PART IV

SUMMING UP

Chapter 6

Implications and Ideas for Thinking about the Future

OVERVIEW

This chapter gathers the thoughts from Chapters 1 through 5 to highlight key ideas and, most importantly, raise key questions for anyone to pursue as we move forward in achieving literacy proficiency. The chapter focuses on several concerns as follows: (1) historical concerns, (2) evaluative concerns, (3) processing concerns, (4) assessment and instructional concerns, (5) technological concerns, (6) development concerns, (7) theoretical concerns about learning and cognition, and (8) obsolescence concerns.

We hope that this chapter gives some closure and insight into the future of achieving literacy proficiency. The chapter is organized around key points and what we believe are good questions based on what we have said in the preceding chapters.

GUIDING QUESTIONS

Can we synthesize everything we have said in each chapter into several key thoughts?
What are the implications of what we say and propose for the future?
What questions do we raise for further research?
What questions do we raise for school and societal practices and expectations?

INTRODUCTION

Making sense of earlier chapters is our goal in Chapter 6. Here, we ask if our original curiosity has been satisfied and if there are implications and insights from our work. We hope in seeking this goal that, we can synthesize key ideas from these chapters that will help us raise interesting and significant questions for the future.

HISTORICAL PERSPECTIVES

The first of our concerns is with ideas about historical perspectives and how they give meaning and context to this work. An overriding concept that has come from synthesizing the historical perspectives that permeate all of the chapters is related to adaptation.

Here, we believe that adaptation will be the key to success in achieving literacy proficiency, which appears to be a major idea of this book. It reflects the evolving concept of literacy from its traditional view to what is emerging in a digital world. It reflects the changes in thinking, instruction, assessment, and professional development that influence any practices in schools or society in general.

We see the need for adaptation as it appears in how the evolution of literacy and the history of education in society are interrelated. This is important because understanding the relationship of historical and societal changes with the views on literacy proficiency is crucial to envisioning the future concept of literacy. These societal changes prompt changes in literacy proficiency requirements and help us make projections for future changes.

The historical perspectives on each aspect of literacy reflect the triggers for change and the parallel evolution of literacy. Some of the triggers for change are as follows: (a) the purpose of instruction, (b) who will receive and benefit from instruction, (c) the purpose of literacy, (d)outside influences, (e) economic conditions, (f) government impetus, (g) universal initiatives, (h) class differences, (i) shifts in the societal power structure, (j) delivery systems available, and (k) dissemination of materials. These triggers for change have been part of earlier chapter discussions in some way.

What is also crucial to understand is that this evolution and the related need for adaptation will continue at an exponential pace because of the related changes in society and, most importantly, the digital world of communication. Not adapting leaves us behind and out of a real system for communication.

EVALUATIVE CONCERNS

A second concern is the level and type of evaluation needed to process all communication. The evaluation of messages permeated every level of literacy proficiency through both traditional and digital forms of communication, where the goal is to determine the sender's credibility and, in turn, the messages. It is key that users of all forms of communication establish the credibility of the source and the validity of the message. This requires users to become the gatekeepers of the messages that they receive.

Tracking evaluation as a concept through types of literacy proficiency helps us to identify when, where, and how evaluation must occur. Such evaluation comes from using specific criteria for encoding messages. This creates a need for analysis, synthesis, and critical thinking to develop an awareness of deceptive practices and intentional manipulation. Such evaluation pushes the receiver to encode text in any form beyond basic or even simple inferential comprehension to determine the value of an idea or a message.

No longer can we be satisfied with having a receiver of any age simply get a basic, literal comprehension of text. We must push for the evaluation of all messages.

PROCESSING CONCERNS

Third, we see the probability of change in how processing communication is changing. We must address questions such as "How if at all, does the reading process change in a digital environment?" and "Does change in pace of changes occur over time?" "Are there plateaus, a pattern of recursiveness, a move forward exponentially, or a need for quiet periods of consolidation?" Answering these questions presents challenges for both researchers and practitioners; however, they are crucial to our understanding of both sending and receiving messages.

We also may see that the digital/digital environment may require an adaptation to the processing of messages and that, over time, change how we process text completely. In turn, this may change patterns and processes of thinking that require different strategies for processing these changes and the accompanying text. We need to raise further questions such as "Do processing strategies change generationally, with individuals, with text format, or with delivery systems?" and "Is the change exponential in pace with new platform development?"

Finally, we think this area of concern is rich for a serious line of research, as suggested by earlier chapters.

ASSESSMENT AND INSTRUCTIONAL CONCERNS

Assessment and instructional models must reflect the changes in literacy proficiency in a digital world and a world of traditional communication. This means that the relationship or distinction between instruction and assessment must be examined. We believe there needs to be a strong coupling of instruction and assessment that may not be reflected in the practices of today. As part of this coupling, we need to look at continuous progress over time rather than specific discrete assessment in a pre–post yearly fashion. Thus, the assessment will need to mirror instruction better.

Instruction and assessment will need to consider the perceptions of both professionals developing and delivering instruction and assessment, as well as the learner/examinee's perceptions of the tasks for assessment and for interpreting the results. Evaluating proficiency also will need to consider processing strategies and levels of understanding beyond basic and simple inferences with consideration of text formats and topics. Scoring schemes and rubrics must be flexible and designed for emerging tasks. In turn, new mathematical models may be needed to justify comparative procedures for assessment tasks and related scoring schemes.

We also need to know who we will choose to instruct for this type of literacy proficiency and assessment. Those providing instruction may have to adapt also. Traditional worksheet-type activities must be changed for more interactive, teacher-guided instruction and support. This may force changes in instruction and curriculum, as well as the selection of materials.

Finally, this area of concern will need a great deal of work and be rich for researching serious questions about assessment. Some of this work is happening and will need to continue.

TECHNOLOGICAL CONCERNS

Technological concerns will be very challenging because of the rate of development, changes, and obsolescence that occur in technology. We must begin with understanding the contributions and challenges of technology in delivery systems to understand the changes in the concept of literacy, its instruction, and its assessment.

We need to answer questions such as "What are those contributions and challenges, and how do they influence the changing concept of literacy?" and "How does technology hinder the development of literacy proficiency?" We then must determine how different uses of technology get used in instruction and assessment with what advantages or disadvantages, and how we can identify future uses. Embracing these changes can help us see how technology can broaden the means for evaluating literacy proficiency and our means for assessing it. It can help us keep abreast of technological advancements—something that must happen.

Finally, we need to research and test the effectiveness of various types of uses of technology given specified goals for achieving literacy proficiency.

DEVELOPMENT CONCERNS

As an outgrowth of Chapters 1–4, we addressed the need for professional development in Chapter 5. There, we considered the who, background knowledge, tools, and guidance for delivering development to those providing instructional and assessment needs. Here, we believe that with the constant changes in technology, instruction, and assessment, we need an open model for professional development to be stable and successful throughout the many changes that will occur over time.

The model must include not only those delivering such services but also how students may participate to have instruction and assessment be interactive in nature. It will be important to consider the length of time for continuous work with those who need guidance as well as a recognition that good frames of periods of consolidation for the development of new skills will be needed. What is also important is that the development be timely and immediately relevant to the receiver, or the time sensitiveness of the material will make for the obsolescence of the development of skills.

For the development to reflect the state-of-the-art practices in developing literacy proficiency, as suggested in this book, those same practices should be incorporated into the instruction in development activities. Professional development has an important part to play in achieving the kind of performance that we hope to achieve in making the populace literate for today's world.

The last two concerns that we will consider here, Theoretical Concerns and Obsolescence, are not ones that were as directly considered in the book; however, we think that they are real concerns as we move forward in identifying the implications of the work in this book.

THEORETICAL CONCERNS ABOUT LEARNING AND COGNITION

What we believe to be important are answers to questions about "Do we need to change models of learning and theories about cognitive processing as we move into the demands of the digital environment?" or "Do we need to re-evaluate aspects of learning theory and cognitive processes employed in literacy activities that may come from the changes in achieving literacy proficiency?" We also need to address any changes in processing messages that may be consequences that influence the way individuals think and learn. What, then, are the pluses and minuses of this activity?

The key question here is, "What learning theories or theories of cognitive processes still have explanatory power for understanding processing and comprehension processes in a digital world?" Although we have not addressed this question directly, the ideas in this book make this an important question for interdisciplinary work in areas such as psychology and neuroscience.

Obsolescence

The last area of concern, and one that we did not address directly, is that of obsolescence. Change may make many present and past practices less desirable or at least less useful. This kind of change will be difficult to face—as with many changes. A key question that has emerged as we moved from face-to-face activity is, "What is the role of social/human contact for learning in these new environments?" Once people moved to remote learning, did we develop the need for a hybrid model for instruction and assessment for delivering and planning our goals and activities? In what ways does the hybrid model make some classroom and societal practices obsolete or improved?

In conjunction with the changes that technology will bring, how will schools compete with the rise of alternative venues for learning, both public and private? We see these venues mushroom as learners become adept at working in a digital world or need less social/human interaction to learn some subjects or skills. This move toward privatizing these services grows. Who will be directing the education of the populace, and in what ways? These are serious questions for educators in all environments to consider.

FINAL THOUGHTS ON THESE CONCERNS

We hope this final chapter has helped you see what seems to be emerging in the thinking on literacy proficiency from various perspectives and that there seem to be as many questions waiting for researchers, practitioners, and learners. We only have hunches about the answers and leave some of this work to you.

Bibliographic References

Adult and Community Learning Services (ACLS). (2022, March). *Digital Literacy in Adult Education*. Massachusetts Department of Elementary and Secondary Education. https://www.doe.mass.edu/acls/frameworks/DigitalLiteracy.html

Akin, J., Goldberg, A., Myers, G., & Stewart, J. (1970). *Language Behavior: A Book of Readings in Communication. For Elwood Murray on the Occasion of His Retirement.* Berlin, Boston: De Gruyter Mouton. https://doi.org/10.1515/9783110878752

Antoninis, M., & Montoya, S. (2018, March 19). A global framework to measure digital literacy. UNESCO: Institute for Statistics. http://uis.unesco.org/en/blog/global-framework-to-measure-digital-literacy

Arnove, R.F., & Graff, H.J. (Ed.). (1987). *National Literacy Campaigns: Historical and Comparative Perspectives.* NY: Plenum Press.

Atwell, N. (2009). *In the Middle.* Portsmouth, NH: Heinemann.

Au, K.H. (2013). Helping high schools meet higher standards. *Journal of Adolescent and Adult Literacy,* 37(3), 267–288.

Au, K.H., & Raphael, T.E. (2011). The staircase curriculum: Whole school collaboration to improve literary achievement. *New England Reading Association Journal,* 46(2), 1–8.

Aulls, M. (1982). *Developing Readers in Today's Elementary Schools.* Boston: Allyn and Bacon.

Balajthy, E. (2007). Technology and current reading/literacy assessment strategies. *The Reading Teacher,* 61(3), 240–247.

Berlo, D. (1960). *The Process of Communication.* New York: Rinehart, & Winston.

Blom, A., Nusat, M., & Goldin, N. (2020, August 10). How to define, measure, and assess digital skills. World Bank Blogs. https://blogs.worldbank.org/arabvoices/how-define-measure-and-assess-digital-skills-0

Borko, H. (2004). Professional development and teacher learning: Mapping the terrain. *Educational Researcher,* 33, 3–15.

Brownell, C.J., & Sheridan, D.M. (2020). Orienting our ears to community: Examining adult-produced field recordings of a living-learning community. *Journal of Adolescent and Adult Literacy,* 64(4), 464–467. https://doi.org/10.1002/jaal.1119

Butler, D., & Schnellert, L. (2012). Collaborative inquiry in teacher professional development. *Teaching and Teacher Education*, 28, 1206–1220.

California Emerging Technology Fund. (2008, November). *California ICT Digital Literacy Assessments and Curriculum Framework*. California Emerging Technology Fund (CETF). https://www.cetfund.org/action-and-results/public-policy-initiatives/digital-literacy/

Calkins, L. (2001). *The Art of Teaching Reading*. New York, NY: Longman Publishers.

Casey, K. (2006). *Literacy Coaching: The Essentials*. Portsmouth, NH: Heinemann.

Cassel, G., & Li, C.C. (1977). Theories of political literacy. *Political Behavior*, 19(4), 317–333.

Castek, J., & Coiro, J. (2015). Understanding what students know: Evaluating their online research and reading comprehension skills. *Journal of Adolescent & Adult Literacy*, 58(7), 546–549. https://doi.org/10.1002/jaal.402

Caulfield, M. (2017). *Web Literacy for Student Fact-Checkers . . . and Other People Who Care about Facts*. Pressbooks. https://webliteracy.pressbooks.com/

Cazden, C. (2001). *Classroom Discourse: The Language of Teaching and Learning*. Portsmouth, NH: Heinemann.

Chen, G.-D., Lee, J.-H., Wang, C.-Y., Chao, P.-Y., Li, L.-Y., & Lee, T.-Y. (2012). An empathic avatar in a computer-aided learning program to encourage and persuade learners. *Journal of Educational Technology & Society*, 15(2), 62–72.

Chetty, K., Shenglin, B., Josie, J., Gcora, N., Liu, O., & Li, W. (2017, April 5). *Bridging the Literacy Divide: Measuring Digital Literacy*. G20-Insights.org. https://www.g20-insights.org/policy_briefs/bridging-literacy-divide-measuring-digital-literacy

Coiro, J. (2003). Exploring literacy on the Internet: Reading comprehension on the internet: Expanding our understanding of reading comprehension to encompass new literacies. *The Reading Teacher*, 56(5), 456–454.

Coward, C., & Fellow, M. (2018). *Digital Skills Toolkit*. International Telecommunication Union (ITU). https://www.itu.int/en/itu-digital skills toolkit

Coward, C., Wedlake, S., Anderson, A., & Teltscher, S. (2020). *Digital Skills Assessment Guidebook*. International Telecommunication Union (ITU). https://www.academy.itu.int/itu-d/projects-activities/research-publications/digital- skills-insights/digital-skills-assessment-guidebook

Cox, C., & Many, J. (1992). Toward an understanding of the aesthetic response to literature. *Language Arts*, 69, 28–35.

Dagostino, L. (1987). The consequences of literacy. *New England Reading Association*, Sturbridge, MA.

Dagostino, L. (1988). The assessment of literacy. *New England Research Association*, Portland, ME.

Dagostino, L. (1991). The implications of a two-tier model of text comprehension for assessment and evaluation. *Eastern Education Research Association*, Boston, MA.

Dagostino, L. (1996). Developing and validating a construct of scientific literacy and thinking. *New England Philosophy of Education Society Conference*, Harvard University, Massachusetts.

Dagostino, L. (2019, August 4–7). Living in a literate world. *21st Nordic International Literacy Conference*, Copenhagen, Denmark.

Dagostino, L., & Carifio, J. (1994a). Establishing the logical validity of instructional activities for teaching reading evaluatively. *Journal of Reading Improvement*, 31(1), 14–21.

Dagostino, L., & Carifio, J. (1994b). *Reading Evaluatively and Literacy: A Cognitive View*. Boston: Allyn and Bacon (out of print).

Dagostino, L., & Carifio, J. (1994c). The attributes of the literate reader in a pluralistic society. *Journal of Reading Improvement*, 31(2), 98–100.

Dagostino, L., & Carifio, J. (1995). Instructional implications of the construct of the context of discourse for literacy education. *Eastern Educational Research Association Conference*, South Carolina.

Dagostino, L., & Carifio, J. (1999). Achieving proficiency in various specialized literacies. *WORK: A Journal of Prevention, Assessment and Rehabilitation*, 13, 83–88.

Dagostino, L., Carifio, J., Bauer, J., & Zhao, Q. (2013). Cross-cultural reading comprehension assessment in Malay and English as it relates to the Dagostino and Carifio model of reading comprehension. *Current Issues in Education*, 16(1), 1–13.

Dagostino, L., Carifio, J., Bauer, J., & Zhao, Q. (2014). Assessment of a reading comprehension instrument as it relates to cognitive abilities as defined by bloom's revised taxonomy. *Current Issues in Education*, 17(1).

Dagostino, L., Deasy, M., & Carifio, J. (2016). The development of the concept of literacy: Post War 1945 into the future. *New England Reading Association Journal*, 51(2), 15–24.

Darling-Hammond, L., & Sykes, G. (1999). *Teaching as the Learning Profession: Handbook of Policy and Practice*. San Francisco: Jossey-Bass.

Deasy, M. (2012). *Developing Basic and Higher Level Reading Processing Skills: Exploring an Instructional Framework with the Progress in International Reading Literacy Study (pirls) 2006 Database*. Unpublished doctoral dissertation. University of Massachusetts Lowell.

Deasy, M., Dagostino, L., Carifio, J., & Fenster, J. (2013). Developing basic and higher level reading processing skill: Exploring an instructional framework with the progress in international reading literacy study 2006 data base. *Northeastern Educational Research Association Conference* – Best Paper and *American Educational Research Association Conference* – Distinguished Paper Award.

Demographics of Social Media Users and Adoption in the United States. (2023, May 11). Pew Research Center: Internet, Science & Tech. https://www.pewresearch.org/internet/fact-sheet/social-media/

DESE MCAS. (2023). Massachusetts Department of Elementary and Secondary Education. MCAS:2022 MCAS Sample Student Work and Scoring Guides. https://doe.mcas.edu/mcas/student/2022/grade8/ela.html

Ertmer, P. (1999). Addressing first- and second-order barriers to change: Strategies for technology integration. *Educational Technology Research and Development*, 47, 47–61. https://doi.org/10.1007/BF02299597

European Commission. (2016). The European digital competence framework for citizens. Publications Office of the European Union.

Eyal, L. (2012). Digital assessment literacy: The core role of the teacher in a digital environment. *Educational Technology & Society*, 15(2), 37–49.

Forzani, E., Corrigan, J.A., & Slomp, D. (2020). Reimagining literacy assessment through a new literacies lens. *Journal of Adolescent & Adult Literacy*, 64(3), 351–355. https://doi.org/10.1002/jaal.1098

Freire, P. (2000). *Pedagogy of the Oppressed* (20th-anniversary ed.). New York: Continuum.

Fullan, M. (1991). *The New Meaning of Educational Change*. New York: Teachers College Press.

Fullan, M. (2000). The three stories of educational reform. *Phi Delta Kappan*, 81, 581–584.

Fullan, M. (2002). *Leadership and Sustainability: Systems Thinkers in Action*. Thousand Oaks, CA: Corwin Press.

Fullan, M. (2014). *The New Meaning of Educational Change* (4th ed.). New York: Teachers College Press.

Furenes, M.I., Kucirkova, N., & Bus, A.G. (2021). A comparison of children's reading on paper versus screen: A meta-analysis. *Review of Educational Research*, 91(4), 483–517. https://doi.org/10.3102/0034654321998074

Giles, C., & Hargreaves, A. (2006). The sustainability of innovative schools as learning organizations and professional learning communities during standardized reform. *Educational Administration Quarterly*, 42(1), 124–156.

Goodman, K. (1986). *What's Whole in Whole Language?* Portsmouth, NH: Heinemann.

Gray, W.S. (1917). Education writings. *The Elementary School Journal*, 18(1), 56–80.

Gray, W.S. (1969). *The Teaching of Reading and Writing: An International Survey*. Chicago: Unesco.

Griffith, P.B., Ruan, J., Steppp, J., & Kimmel, S. (2014). The design and implementation of effective professional development in elementary and early childhood settings. In L.E. Martin, S. Kragler, D. Quatroche, & K. Bauserman (Eds.), *Handbook of Professional Development in Education: Successful Models and Practices, PreK-12* (pp. 189–204). New York: The Guilford Press.

Hackman, R.J. (2002). *Leading Teams: Setting the Stage for Great Performances*. Boston: Harvard Business School Press.

Henry, L.A., Castek, J., O'Byrne, W.I., & Zawilinski, L. (2012). Using peer collaboration to support online reading, writing, and communication: An empowerment model for struggling readers. *Reading & Writing Quarterly: Overcoming Learning Difficulties*, 28(3), 279–306.

Hodges, H.L.B. (1996). Using research to inform practice in urban schools: Ten key strategies to success. *Educational Policy*, 10, 223–252.

Huey, E. (1908). *The Psychology and Pedagogy of Reading*. The Macmillan Company. Retrieved from google scholar https://books.google.com

International Society for Technology in Education (ISTE). (2022). *Digital Literacy Assessments*. https://www.iste.org/standards/seal-of-alignmnet/digital-literacy-assessment

Jacobs, J., & Yendol-Hoppey, D. (2014). Using action research to target and generate professional learning. In L.E. Martin, S. Kragler, D. Quatroche, & K.

Bauserman (Eds.), *Handbook of Professional Development in Education: Successful Models and Practices, PreK-12* (pp. 304–319). New York: The Guilford Press.

Johnson, P.E. (1967). Some psychological aspects of subject-matter structure. *Journal of Educational Psychology*, 58(2) 75–8.

Johnston-Parsons, M. (2012). *Dialogue and Difference in a Teacher Education Program: A 16-Year Sociocultural Study of a Professional Development School.* Charlotte, NC: Information Age Publishing.

Joyce, B., & Showers, B. (1995). *Student Achievement through Staff Development: Fundamentals of School Renewal.* White Plains, NY: Longman.

Joyce, B., & Showers, B. (2002). *Student Achievement through Staff Development.* Washington, DC: Association for Supervision & Curriculum Development.

Karpati, A. (2011). Policy brief: Digital literacy in education. UNESCO Institute for Information Technologies in Education. UNESDOC Digital Library: https://unesdoc.unesco.org/ark/48223/pf0000214485

Keene, E., & Zimmerman, S. (2007). *Mosaic of Thought: The Power of Comprehension Strategy Instruction.* Portsmouth, NH: Heinemann.

Krashen, S. (2004). *The Power of Reading: Insights from the Research* (2nd ed.). Portsmouth, NH: Heinemann.

Lammers, J.C., & Astuti, P. (2020). Calling for a global turn to inform digital literacies education. *Journal of Adolescent and Adult Literacy*, 64(4), 371–177. https://doi.org/10.1002/jaal.1103

Law, N., Woo, D., de la Torre, J., & Wong, G. (2018). *A Global Framework of Reference on Digital Literacy Skills for Indicator 4.4.2: Information Paper No. 51.* Montreal, Quebec: UNESCO Institute for Statistics.

LeBlanc, C., & Dagostino, L. (2015, October 25). What counts as literacy: Broadening our vision of visual representation. *New England Philosophy of Education Society Conference*, New Britain, Connecticut.

Leu, D.J., Coiro, J., Castek, J., Hartman, D., Henry, L.A., & Reinking, D. (2008). Research on instruction and assessment in the new literacies of online reading comprehension. In C. Collins Block & S. Parris (Eds.), *Comprehension Instruction: Research-based Best Practices* (pp. 321–346). Guilford Press.

Leu, D., Kinzer, C., Coiro, J., Castek, J., & Henry, L. (2013). New literacies: A dual-level theory of the changing nature of literacy, instruction and assessment. In D.E. Alvermann, N.J. Unrau, & R.B Rudell (Eds.), *Theoretical Models and Processes of Reading* (6th ed., pp. 1150–1181). International Reading Association.

Leu, D., Kulikowich, J., Sedransk, N., & Coiro, J. (2013, June 7). *ORCA: Online Research and Comprehension Assessment.* Neag School of Education -University of Connecticut. http://orca/uconn.edu.org

Lieberman, A., & Miller, L. (2014). Teachers as professionals: Evolving Definitions of staff Development. In L.E. Martin, S. Kragler, D. Quatroche, & K. Bauserman (Eds.), *Handbook of Professional Development in Education: Successful Models and Practices, PreK-12* (pp. 3–21). New York: The Guilford Press.

Lind, A. (2008). *Literacy for All: Making a Difference.* Paris: United Nations Educational, Scientific and Cultural Organization.

Literacy Information and Communication System (LINCS). (2022). *Teaching Skills that Matter: Digital Literacy.* LINCS- in association with the U.S. Department of Education, Office of Career, Technical, and Adult Education (OCTAE). https://lincs.ed.gov/state-resources/federal-initiatives/teaching-skills-matter-adult-education/digital-literacy

Lyons, C., & Pinnell, G.S. (2001). *Systems for Change in Literacy Education: A Guide to Professional Development.* Portsmouth, NH: Heinemann.

Martin, L.E., Kragler, S., Quatroche, D., & Bauserman, K. (Eds.). (2014). *Handbook of Professional Development in Education: Successful Models and Practices, PreK-12.* New York: The Guilford Press.

Martin, M.O., Mullis, I.S., & Foy, P. (2015). Assessment design for PIRLS, PIRLS literacy, and ePIRLS in 2016. In Michael O. Martin, Ina V.S. Mullis, & Pierre Foy (Eds.), *PIRLS 2016 Assessment Framework* (2nd ed.). Retrieved from Boston College, TIMSS & PIRLS International Study Center website: https://timssandpirls.bc.edu/pirls2016/framework.html

Maslow, A.H. (1987). *Motivation and Personality.* NY: Harper and Row.

McLuhan, M. (1964). *Understanding Media: The Extensions of Man.* New York: McGraw-Hill.

Morris, S., & Stommel, J. (2023). *An Urgency of Teachers: The Work of Critical Pedagogy.* North Haven, CT: Hybrid Press, Inc.

Mortensen, C. David. (1972). *Communication: The Study of Human Interaction.* McGraw-Hill.

Mullis, I.V.S., & Martin, M.O. (Eds.). (2015). *PIRLS 2016 Assessment Framework* (2nd ed.). Retrieved from Boston College, TIMSS & PIRLS International Study Center website: https://timssandpirls.bc.edu/pirls2016/framework.html

Mullis, I.V.S., & Martin, M.O. (2019). *PIRLS 2021 Assessment Frameworks.* Chestnut Hill, MA: TIMSS & PIRLS International Study Center International & Association for the Evaluation of Educational Achievement (IEA).

Mullis, I.V.S., & Martin, M.O. (Eds.). (2019). *PIRLS 2021 Assessment.* Retrieved from Boston College, TIMSS & PIRLS International Study Center website: https://timssandpirlsFrameworks.bc.edu/pirls2021/frameworks/

Murray, J. (2020, August 16). *How to Assess Digital Literacy for Students (and Educators!). National Education Association.* https://www.nea.org/advocating-for-change/new-from-nea/how-assess-digital-literacy-studnets-and-educators

New Meridian Resource Center. (2023). ELA test design: ELA/literacy scoring rubrics. https://resources.newmeridiancorp.org/ela-test-design/

Organization for Economic Co-operation and Development (OECD). (2015). *Students, Computers and Learning: Making the Connection.* PISA, OECD Publishing. http://dx.doi.org/10.1787/9789264239555-en

Organization for Economic Co-operation and Development (OECD). (2021). *21st-Century Readers: Developing Literacy Skills in a Digital World.* Paris: PISA, OECD Publishing. https://doi.org/10.1787/a83d84cb-en

Organization for Economic Co-operation and Development (OECD). (2022). *Program for International Student Assessment: Try PISA questions.* Retrieved July 2022 https://www.oecd.org/pisa/test

Panhwar, F. (2020). Functions of code-switching in a private chat on Facebook: Dr Farida Yasmin Panhwar. *Journal of English Language, Literature and Education*, 1, 16. https://doi.org/10.54692/jelle.2020.01045

Pearson, P.D., & Gallagher, M.C. (1983). The instruction of reading comprehension. *Contemporary Educational Psychology*, 8, 317–344.

Pearson, P.D., & Hamm, D.N. (2005). The assessment of reading comprehension: A review of practices: Past, present, and future. In S.G. Paris & S.A. Stahl (Eds.), *Children's Reading Comprehension and Assessment* (pp. 13–69). Lawrence Erlbaum Associates.

Peng, P., Lee, K., Li, J.L., Li, S., Joshi, R.M., & Tao, S. (2021). Simple view of reading in Chinese: A one-stage meta-analytic structural equation modeling. *Review of Educational Research*, 91(1), 3–33. https://doi.org/10.3102/0034654320964198

Perkins, D. (1993). Teaching for understanding. *American Educator: The Professional Journal of the American Federation of Teachers*, 17, 28–35.

Peterson, R. (1992). *Life in a Crowded Place: Making a Learning Community*. Portsmouth, NH: Heinemann.

Prest, P., & Prest, J. (1988). Theory into practice: Clarifying our intentions: Some thoughts on the application of Rosenblatt's transactional theory of reading in the classroom. *English Quarterly*, 21, 127–133.

Probst, R.E. (2004). *Response and Analysis: Teaching Literature in the Secondary School*. Portsmouth, NH: Heinemann.

Rework America Business Network. (2019). *Digital Blindspot: How Digital Literacy can Create a more Resilient American Workforce*. Markle Foundation.

Richardson, V., & Placier, P. (2001). Teacher change. In V. Richardson (Ed.), *Handbook of Research on Teaching* (4th ed., pp. 905–950). Washington, DC: American Educational Research Association.

Routman, R. (2002). *Reading Essentials: The Specifics you Need to Teach Reading Well*. Portsmouth, NH: Heinemann.

Rowell, S. (2007). Professional development is union work: Embedding the standards. *Journal of Staff Development*, 28(1), 59–60.

Ruday, S., & Caprino, K. (2023). *Student-Centered Literacy Assessment: An Asset-based Approach*. Routledge.

Sarason, S.B. (1990). *The Predictable Failure of Educational Reform: Can We Change the Course Before It's Too Late?* San Francisco: Jossey-Bass.

Scammacca, N., Roberts, G., Cho, E., Williams, K., Roberts, G., Vaughn, S., & Carroll, M. (2016). A century of progress: Reading interventions for students in grades 6–12, 1914–2014, *Review of Educational Research*, 86(3), 756–800.

Schmidt, A. (2014). *Between The Languages: Code-Switching in Bilingual Communication*. Anchor Academic Publishing.

Schrock, K. (2023, July 6). Assessment and rubrics. Kathy Schrock's Guide to Everything. https://www.schrockguide.net/assessment-and-rubrics.html

Scot, T., Callahan, C., & Urquhardt, J. (2009). Paint by number teachers and cookie-cutter students: The unintended effects of high-stakes testing on the education of gifted students. *Roeper Review*, 31, 40–52.

Simon, J. (1956). The teaching of reading and writing: An international survey. *The Elementary School Journal*, 57(2), 83–94.

Smylie, M.A. (1995). Teacher learning in the workplace: Implications for school reform. In T.R. Guskey & M. Hubberman (Eds.), *Professional Development in Education: New Paradigms and Practices* (pp. 92–113). New York: Teachers College Press.

Song, J. (2019). Language socialization and code-switching: A case study of a Korean-English bilingual child in a Korean translational family. *International Journal of Bilingual Education and Bilingualism*, 22(2), 91–106. https://doi.org/10.1080/13670050.2016.1231165

Sticht, T.G. (Ed.). (1975). *Reading for Working: A Functional Literacy Anthology*. Alexandria, VA: HumRRo.

Sticht, T.G. (1995). The military experience and workplace literacy: A review and synthesis for policy and practice. National Center on Adult Literacy technical Report TR 94-01. March 1995. google scholar https://citeseerx.ist.psu.edu/document?repid=rep1&type=pdf&doi=14731d7bd7aaecb85768d0e1e629258af84fca6f

Sticht, T.G., & Caylor, J.S. (1971, December). Development and evaluation of job reading task tests. *Journal of Literacy Research*, 4(4), 29–50.

Sticht, T.G., & Kern, R.P. (1970, December). Project realistic: Determining literacy demands of jobs. *Journal of Literacy Research*, 2(3), 191–212.

Tallerico, M. (1995). *Leading Curriculum Improvement: Fundamentals for School Principals*. Lanham, MD: Rowman & Littlefield.

The Nations Report Card. (2023). Data tools: Question tool. https://www.nationsreportcard.gov/nqt/searchquestions

TIMSS & PIRLS International Study Center. (2022). *E-pirls: Take the e-pirls Assessment*. Retrieved July 2022 https://pirls2016.org/epirls/take-the-epirls-assessment

Toll, C. (2018). *Educational Coaching: A Partnership for Problem Solving*. Alexandria, VA: Association for Supervision and Curriculum Development.

UNESCO. (2003). *Literacy, a UNESCO Perspective*. Paris: United Nations Educational, Scientific and Cultural Organization.

UNESCO. (2005). *Education for all Global Monitoring Report 2006: Literacy for Life*. Paris: United Nations Educational, Scientific and Cultural Organization.

UNESCO. (2008). *Implementation of the International Plan of Action for the United Nations Literacy Decade: Report of the Director General of the United Nations Educational, Scientific, and Cultural Organization*. Retrieved from http://www.unesco.org/literacy/unld-mid-decade-review

UNESCO-Scott Foresman and Company. Retrieved from UNESCO Digital Library: https://unesdoc.unesco.org/ark:/48223/pf0000002929

US Department of Education. (2021). *Reading Framework for the 2026 National Assessment of Education Progress*. US Dept of Education. Retrieved from https://www.nagb.gov/naep-subject-areas/reading/framework-archive/2026-reading-framework.html

Vosoughi, S., Roy, D., & Aral, S. (2018). The spread of true and false news online. *Science*, 1151(3), 1146–1151.

Vygotsky, L.S. (1978). *Mind in Society: The Development of Higher Psychological Processes*. Cambridge, MA: Harvard University Press.

Weaver, C. (2009). *Reading Process and Practice* (3rd ed.). Portsmouth, NH: Heinemann.

Williams, D. (December 2007/January 2008). Changing classroom practice. *Educational Leadership*, 65(4), 36–42.

World Education Inc. (2022, June 29). Selecting an assessment for digital literacy. *World Education*. https://worlded.org/selecting-an-assessment-for-digital-literacy

Wry, E., & Mullis, I.V.S. (2023). Developing the PIRLS 2021 achievement instruments. In M. von Davier, I.V.S. Mullis, B. Fishbein, & P. Foy (Eds.), *Methods and Procedures: PIRLS 2021 Technical Report* (pp. 1.1–1.24). Boston College: TIMSS & PIRLS International Study Center. https://doi.org/10.6017/lse.tpisc .tr2101.kb7549

About the Authors

Dr. Lorraine Dagostino, professor emeritus at the University of Massachusetts Lowell, has been an educator since 1970 in public schools, community colleges, four-year colleges, and the university. She received her degrees from Russell Sage College, the College of St. Rose, and Syracuse University. Her teaching in the public school was in history, English and Reading. In the community college, she taught study skills classes for college preparation. At the college and university, her work has been in many aspects of reading instruction and theory, along with literacy research studies with graduate students at the Masters and Doctoral levels of study. She has published numerous journal articles and books in these areas of study and was awarded best paper awards from Northeast Educational Research Association (NERA), Eastern Educational Research Association (EERA) and distinguished papers from American Educational Research Association (AERA). She has presented professional papers at State, Regional, National, and International Conferences. Her last book, *Guiding Instruction in Young Adult Literature*, was published in 2021. She has been president of the New England Philosophy of Education Society and the Massachusetts Association of Reading Educators. She also did work at Harvard University as a Research Associate. Her personal interests are traveling and swimming, along with volunteer work for various organizations. She is a Paul Harris fellow from Rotary International.

Dr. Jennifer Bauer is the chair of the Communication, Art, & Design Department at Middlesex Community College in Massachusetts. She was an equity fellow for the Center for Urban Education in 2021. Before MCC, she taught at Lowell High School in Massachusetts for twelve years, as well as summer teaching positions with MS[2] at Phillips Academy Andover and Urban Scholars at the University of Massachusetts, Boston. She also spent fifteen years coaching crew at the middle school, high school, collegiate, and masters levels. Dr. Bauer is an award-winning blogger and filmmaker and has had her writing published online at the Huffington Post, Outdoor Families Magazine, the Bump, and the National Park Foundation. She earned a BS in Video Production from Ithaca College, an MFA in Film Production from Boston University, an MEd in Curriculum and Instruction from Pennsylvania State University, a PhD in literacy studies from the University of Massachusetts, Lowell, and a certificate in Diversity and Inclusion from Cornell University. Her published work and conference papers focus on the educational inequities faced by English Language Learners in the classroom, language variation, and code-switching. Her last book, *Guiding Instruction in Young Adult Literature*, was published in 2021. In her free time, she spends time hiking and camping with her wife and kids and way too much time watching television and movies.

Dr. Michael Deasy is a Reading Specialist in the Athol-Royalston Regional School District in Massachusetts. He received his BA from St. Anselm College, MEd in Elementary Education from Bridgewater State College, CAGS in Reading and Language and EdD in Language Arts and Literacy from the University of Massachusetts Lowell, and a Graduate Certificate in Digital Literacy from the University of Rhode Island. He has presented on literacy topics at the New England Educational Research Organization (NEERO), the Northeast Educational Research Association (NERA), the Eastern Educational Research Association (EERA), the New England Philosophy of Education Society (NEPES), and the American Educational Research Association (AERA). He has been awarded the best paper award from NERA, presented at a distinguished paper session at AERA, and published in the Journal of the New England Reading Association. His current research interests include literacy acquisition, writing development, and supporting literacy development through digital tools and experiences.

Dr. Kathleen Ryan received a BA from Boston College in English, an MA from the University College Dublin, Ireland, in Anglo-Irish Literature, an MEd from Boston College in Language and Literacy, and an EdD in Language Arts and Literacy from the University of Massachusetts Lowell. She is a professor at Hellenic College in Brookline, MA Dr. Ryan is the co-director of the Literature and History Department and the director of the Education Program, which offers a Minor in Education. Dr. Ryan joined the Hellenic College faculty in 2004 with a wide range of experience in Literature and Literacy. Her past work experiences include the positions of Literacy Specialist and Literacy Coach in public schools and with young adults in public housing developments. Her research focuses on the power of literature to transform both academic and personal lives. Her presentations and publications focus on the importance of nurturing personal responses to literature. Her last book, *Guiding Instruction in Young Adult Literature*, was published in 2021. Her research reflects her belief in the power of literature and its capacity to serve as an agent of empathy, insight, and compassion. Throughout her career, her research and teaching have been shaped by a belief in the transformative power of teaching, learning, and literature.